LEADER BY CHOICE
7 Decisions That Spark Your Purpose, Passion, And Perseverance

by

Andres Valdes

Thank you so much for purchasing my first book. Please download a copy of the free accompanying workbook so you can write your answers to the questions in one place.

Go here:

www.leaderbychoice.me/resources

Disclaimer

The information published in this book represents the author's opinions, personal research, and life experiences. The opinions expressed in this book are the author's own and do not reflect the view of his employer, the Department of State, or the United States government.

Since the success of anyone depends upon the skill and ability of the person, the author makes no guarantees and disclaims any personal loss or liabilities that may occur as a result of the use the information contained herein.

The author tried to recreate events, locales and conversations from my memories of them. In order to maintain their anonymity in some instances I have changed the names of individuals and places, I may have changed some identifying characteristics and details such as physical properties, occupations and places of residence.

Paperback editions
ISBN-13:978-0999164501
ISBN-10:0999164503

Cover design by Jasmine Womack, 31 Publishing

TABLE OF CONTENTS

DEDICATION

To my parents—Pedro and Yasmina—for giving me life.

FOREWORD

There is something to be said about someone who writes based on personal experiences as opposed to theoretical lessons on the topic of leadership. I often come across very ambitious, articulate, charismatic speakers and authors who teach principles by using information they have learned from successful people. But in this case Andres decided to write a book about being and becoming a "Leader by Choice." I would not cosign a book written from the perspective of theory; I can only cosign successful application, and I personally know that Andres has used his personal experiences to transform his life and if applied, it can transform yours.

I remember the first time meeting Andres at a hotel restaurant in Miami, Florida. There were two things that stuck out for me; his humility and his cell phone. Andres has a quiet calm about him that lets you know he has been through some storms in his life but has not remained in them. I always say, "If you can't let go of what happened you'll never be ready for what's coming." His humility lets me know he is ready for what's coming.

The other thing that stood out for me was his cell phone. I was amazed that he was using a "flip phone," without Internet that had to be at least five years old. This amazed me because in this day of the iPhone he was using a phone that most of us would say is "old and outdated." However, for me this spoke volumes about his leadership and not allowing "life" to dictate how he chooses to live. As I have come to know and respect Andres over the years, I can now say that he is not just a leader, but someone with a life story which motivates others to lead. He walks the talk and practices what he "preaches."

I recommend this book to all. It is filled with leadership principles and life tips that are born out of life experiences and presented in a way that is appealing, gripping, and educational.

As it has been said: "To whom much is given, much is required." To Andres, much has been given and experienced, and thus it is required of you to share and continue to be a Leader by Choice.

Kendall Ficklin
CEO and Founder of GRINDATION

INTRODUCTION

"Your father's dead!"

Those were the first words I heard as I walked through the door of my best friend JC's house. I found myself gasping for air after listening to those three words. Feeling like someone had punched me, I held my stomach and bent over gasping for the little air I could collect.

JC's mom was somehow given the responsibility of breaking the news to me of my father's question-filled and unexpected death earlier in the day.

As Mike Tyson said, "Everyone has a plan till they get punched in the mouth."[1] The news of my father's death was definitely one of those punches. The pain from his death was unbearable at times. After this experience, I thought that there would be some limit or cap on the amount of crappy stuff that life threw at me.

The reality is everyone gets punched in the mouth by life and for most of us, including myself, we get hit more than once.

1

I'll share some of those experiences later, but I don't want to portray my experiences into some bigger deal then they were. I now realize how we get through stuff is more important than what we go through.

There have been times in my past where I felt like the world was completely against me and was trying to count me out.

Have you ever felt that way?

During the most difficult times, I felt like I had an excuse to give up, settle, or become a negative statistic. After all, I felt life was doing an excellent job of intentionally keeping me down right from the beginning.

But this book isn't about my struggles. And I'm not looking for sympathy because I'm sure you've been through your own struggles. I'm sure you've had your fair share of punches in the mouth too. You might be going through something right now.

So this book is really about YOU. Surprise!

After all, so many people in this world are born into circumstances where the odds are stacked against them and making it out or having any type of success seems impossible.

Some of us have been through so much we don't believe happiness or good things can come our way. It may feel like nothing you do is working, so you're not sure what to do next and are thinking of giving it all up.

Maybe you're still affected by the loss of a parent or a loved one. Or maybe you've been through verbal, physical, or drug abuse and can't shake your past or feel unworthy of success, achievement, or a great life.

Some people find themselves unfulfilled, directionless, and lacking daily motivation.

And some people have done all the right things, but haven't found work that engages them and are worried about never living up to their highest purpose and potential.

This book is for people, who regardless of their circumstances, feel stuck and unsure of the direction they're headed, but want to do something.

I overcame some of these experiences so I wrote this book to show you that it is possible to lead yourself in a different direction even when you don't have all the answers and you feel like throwing in the towel.

Sometimes it's hard for me to believe my own story. I'm the same kid who was kicked out of high school for being too far behind academically, was arrested at 17, and lived in a clothing factory with his grandparents, and did a bunch of dumb things. But I still

3

managed to get a college degree, complete a graduate degree from my dream school, Columbia University, speak multiple languages, lead teams with hundreds of people, and get to speak about leadership to international audiences.

And now I'm an author.

The best part is I'm just getting started even though I'm turning 40 this year. But I'm not trying to impress you. I want you to know that it's not too early or too late to start to make positive changes. The place you started does not determine that place you finish.

I simply want to encourage you to find and achieve **your** vision of success. Author, speaker, and business owner Zig Ziglar said, "Money will buy you a bed, but not a good night's sleep, a house, but not a home, a companion, but not a friend."[2]

Understanding true success matters.

The philosophy I'm going to share is not some long lost "secret to success." It's just an easily learned skill, but you'll need to put in effort and practice before you can benefit from it.

You have everything you need to get started.

The biggest changes in life come from the smallest adjustments. Most of the time these are unnoticeable in the moment, but when added over time they completely change our life's direction.

4

The big, yet simple, idea you will learn in this book is this: you have the power to completely change the direction of your life. But first you have to accept that your life won't change until you take responsibility for changing it.

And this change will happen when you decide to become a Leader by Choice.

A Leader by Choice is someone who intentionally decides and commits to stop living passively and starts actively pursuing their best life possible through self-leadership.

A Leader by Choice makes intentional decisions that put them on the path to pre-defined success in key areas of life. They pursue achievements in areas they feel are the most important and not ones defined by other people, fear, or common culture.

You were created to lead, regardless of your age, gender or looks. And it doesn't matter what you do for a living.

Let me clarify something else. There's nothing wrong with you. You're not broken, and I'm not here to fix you.

My intention is to upgrade your overall philosophy and perspective on life, so you're in a position to win or learn at all times.

But no matter how many motivational videos you watch, or how many inspirational stories you read, or how many great ideas you have, at the end of the day, it all comes down to one thing.

Execution.

We generally have great intentions at the beginning of any journey, but things happen along the way. We lose hope, get distracted, or get punched in the mouth by life. These happenings set us on a different course.

Unfortunately, having good intentions is not enough. And now I have to warn you about something: Whenever you try making improvements in your life, take risks that promise to elevate you, or pursue something creative, you'll be visited by this thing called self-doubt.

Any thoughts, ideas, or excuses that are trying to convince you to stop this journey of self-discovery and self-improvement are just visits from self-doubt or "resistance." Steven Pressfield said, "Most of us have two lives: the life we live, and the unlived life within us. Between the two stands resistance."[3]

You can overcome the resistance. If others have done it, so can you. But what you are about to learn is something so simple it's deceptive. I almost missed it myself.

Over a year into writing this book, I wasn't 100% certain on the central theme. Then one day in a leadership lecture I was giving, one of the participants, a young lady named Hasmic, asked me what was it that caused me to change the direction of my life. I mumbled something, but I don't even remember what I said.

It bothered me that I couldn't give her a clear answer, so I kept thinking about it. That evening and in the following days, her question kept floating in my head. A few days later I had one of those eureka moments.

Her question helped me realize that at the core of my life's changes was not one, but several critical choices I made. And each one shifted my trajectory slightly like that of an aircraft carrier slightly shifting course.

These are the seven decisions I made. You can choose to make them too:

1. Choose Your Story:
   You will learn how to create a new story that is empowering instead of limiting.

2. Choose To Know Thyself:
   You will learn how to manage weaknesses and leverage your strengths.

3. Choose Your Attitude:
   You will learn how to adopt a winning attitude regardless of your circumstances.

4. Choose To Lead:
   You will discover your unique leadership style.

5. Choose Your Mission:
   You will learn how to create a personal mission that pushes you to excellence and keeps you motivated.

6. Choose To Grow:
   You will learn how to close the gap between the person you are today and the person you dream of becoming.

7. Choose To Overcome:
   You will learn how to turn your setbacks into fuel for something greater.

I now realize that collectively these decisions were so powerful because they have to do with three things:

1. Purpose
2. Passion
3. Perseverance

Going with the flow of life and hoping everything turns out fine is a not a plan. That's what I call leading by chance.

This isn't just a book. It's an opportunity to reflect and get clarity on what you really want. That's why at the end of each chapter, there are questions for you to journal. You can record your answers in a free workbook available at www.leaderbychoice.com/resources.

Did you know you have 1,440 minutes in a day?

Can you spare 15 minutes per day for this book?

Don't you owe it yourself to see how much you can accomplish and experience with your life?

Then don't let resistance get in your way. Commit to reading and doing the exercises. Tell someone who is close to you that you're going to finish reading this book, do the exercises, and then you'll share what you learned with them.

Why? Because then you'll have someone expecting you to come through. This creates good pressure.

My promise to you is that when you finish reading this book and do the exercises, you're going to be empowered to make seven seemingly small decisions that will have the potential to change the trajectory of your life.

Let's finish this section with a poem I read recently. It's written on the tomb of an Anglican Bishop in the crypts of Westminster Abbey, in London.

"When I was young and free, and my imagination had no limits, I dreamed of changing the world. As I grew older and wiser, I discovered the world would not change, so I shortened my sights somewhat and decided to change only my country.

But, it too, seemed immovable.

As I grew into my twilight years, in one last desperate attempt, I settled for changing only my family, those closest to me, but alas, they would have none of it.

And now as I lie on my deathbed, I suddenly realize: If I had only changed myself first, then by example I would have changed my family.

From their inspiration and encouragement, I would then have been able to better my country and, who knows, I may have even changed the world."

Chapter 1
CHOOSE YOUR STORY

"We have more control than most of us realize. Each day is filled with thousands of opportunities to change the story of our lives."
Michael Hyatt

From great books to inspiring speeches, to Hollywood and even the video game industry, the power of storytelling is everywhere. Nothing can capture our imagination, attention, and money like an engaging narrative. Some stories are so powerful they become a part of us, whether we know it or not. Stories draw us into them. Some can hold us hostage, and others can set us free.

There's no doubt in my mind we are living powerful stories. But are you living one of your own choosing or one that was written for you? We were all born into some narrative that existed before we came along.

The story of Roger Bannister's history-making mile race is well known and often repeated. There's a reason for that. Bannister's victory demonstrated the extraordinary power of the human mind and our imagination.

Let's review what happened.

Before 1954, it was commonly believed in sports that running a mile in under four minutes was physically impossible. And according to physiologists, it was not only impossible but also physically dangerous to run that fast. The record at the time was 4:01.04 and could not be broken.

Runners had tried, but as close as they came, they couldn't beat that record. The unbeatable four-minute mark was a line that couldn't be crossed. All athletes accepted this, except for one.

Roger Bannister had not been a stand-out runner. He did not do well in his first Olympic competition, despite high expectations. After returning home, he went to medical school. He could have quit running altogether to focus on his medical studies, but he had unfinished business on the track. He set an audacious goal: to run a mile under four minutes.

Bannister found a new coach, two running partners, and a new training routine. Every day, he used his 90-minute lunch break to train. After improving his time by a full second over the course of one year, he was confident that the four-minute mark could be broken.

Nearly two years after his failure at the Olympics, on May 6, 1954, Bannister ran the mile in 3 minutes, 59.4 seconds. After crossing the finish line in total exhaustion, Bannister said, "pain overtook me. I felt like an exploded flashlight with no will to live."[4]

He'd won, while doing something no one had ever done. And yet he'd only taken two seconds off the previous record. But the aftermath of this race put a spotlight on high achievement and truly showed the power of a mental image and potential.

But this story doesn't end there. By 1957 some 16 runners had clocked in at less than four minutes. What caused so many athletes to do what was considered physically impossible just months earlier?

Like the punching of a glass wall, the story, which became a belief that a mile couldn't be run under four minutes, was obliterated by Bannister. Bannister busted through a psychological wall the runners believed was physical and in doing so he gave them a new story to pursue.

When I deconstructed Bannister's incredible athletic accomplishment, I see it all started with one thing: a decision. It was a crazy one, but Bannister decided that he would be the one to break the record, even if it was considered impossible by the experts. This decision is something I've found in so many people who accomplish extraordinary things, break the status quo, or achieve their dreams no matter the size. At some point in their lives, they chose to live out their own stories instead of settling for a "reality" imposed on them by failures, self-imposed limitations, or culture.

The stories we tell ourselves and accept shape our perspective, which forms our "reality" and determine how far we can see ourselves going. These stories define the actions we can and cannot take. The scariest part about this is that whether we know it or not, we are living in a glass box of the stories we choose to believe for ourselves. Our families, communities, and even countries created these stories. All these things help shape the narrative into which we live and think.

My Old Story

Like Roger Bannister, my parents have a record of their own. They divorced while I was still crawling on my hands and knees, making this a record-setting divorce (in my book). They were married when my mother was in high school, and my father had just started playing basketball for a local community college in Miami. Not only were my parents immature and unprepared, but most importantly they were unwilling to assume responsibility for me. As far back as I can remember I have lived with my paternal grandparents.

I'm not sure when or why my parents divorced since they never talked to me about it and I never asked. And for some reason, neither of my parents took me back even when I got older. Deep down inside of me, I was holding on to resentment and feelings of abandonment which to be honest are still there, but under control.

I always stayed in contact with my parents though, and I saw my father mostly on weekends, but we never really had much quality time. I loved and admired him. I wanted to be just like him, even though he never seemed to have much time to invest in me, so I was unknowingly hungry for his attention and affirmation growing up. His priorities, though, were money, women, and friends. Family came in dead last to everything else.

Despite my father's disinterest, my grandmother taught me to love and respect him. Unfortunately, his life was one long drama scene, which added to my confusion of how I felt about him because I really wanted to be like him and for him to be proud of me. I also wanted a closer relationship with him. He wasn't the type of father to say, "I love you," take me fishing, or have quality time. He just did his own thing and if I was lucky, he'd let me come along for the ride. I also wanted him to be proud of me so in some ways I feel like there's a small part of me, which is still trying to win his approval.

While living with my grandparents, we lost our home on more than one occasion. Once it was due to a fire in which my grandfather suffered third-degree burns on over 90% of his body, but by some miracle of God, he survived. The recovery process, which included one year in the hospital, was brutal on him and difficult for those of us caring for him. We didn't have property insurance, so we lost that home without any form of compensation. Then we moved in with other family members until we could afford to get our own place again.

A few years later, and during the longest stretch without our own home which was two years, we lived in my grandmother's small clothing factory because we couldn't afford our place anymore. My grandmother had built up a small business in Miami's Little Havana neighborhood. For a number of years, she helped larger clothing companies when they had projects they couldn't complete on their own.

My grandmother worked like an animal; I never saw her take a vacation. She came to the United States from Cuba with four children and a few possessions on a Saturday and was working in a factory the following Monday.

Eventually, she closed up as more work was outsourced abroad, but I'm so grateful she had this small business because it literally became our home and only source of income. The business brought in just enough to get us food, clothing, and shelter. And thank goodness for free school lunches!

In the morning, I'd walk to Citrus Grove Middle School then after class, my friends and I would go hang out or play street football. In the evenings, I'd pretend to be going home, but I was really going back to the factory.

I slept on a twin-sized mattress laid out on the floor nestled between wall-to-wall sewing machines, cutting tables, and our pets— disgusting rats that loved chewing on fabric scraps at night. The females chewed the pieces of fabric to make nests for more disgusting rats. Unfortunately, this wasn't the last time our housing situation was unstable. But I never heard any complaining; we just kept going.

Daddy Issues

Adding to the confusion and instability of our lives, no one talked about my father's "day job." At the time, nearly all the men I came in contact with were involved in some type of criminal activity, from drug dealing to underground gambling, including my father. No one ever told me what he did for a living; it wasn't something we talked about over dinner.

But eventually, I figured it out.

When family friends or relatives would disappear for long stretches and no one would tell me what happened, but it normally meant they were in jail. At home, we had a strict unspoken code which is best summarized as "You don't know nothing; you don't see nothing." As a kid who adored his father, this was a confusing situation because I was taught that drugs and criminal life was wrong, but at the same time that's what I was witnessing.

We didn't spend much time together, but I was still crazy about him. At that time, quality time consisted of my father taking me to McDonald's. Drive-through!

Once he picked me up out of the blue. He never said where we were going. He pulled up next to a parked car and then asked me to drive the car we were riding in and to follow him to the mechanic shop he owned. The fact that I was around 12 years old didn't bother him at all.

He didn't fear the law.

My father lived in extremes. He was either broke or he was ball'n. He was constantly borrowing money from his mother. And when he was absolutely desperate, he'd ask to borrow my $100 welfare check, which came the 1st of the month. I hated lending my father money. It wasn't the money I cared about; I just felt humiliated and embarrassed for him. I never asked him how he earned his money, but as a teenager it was clear that it wasn't legal.

My father's brother, who lived with us for a long time, was addicted to drugs, alcohol, and gambling during this time. He was pretty much addicted to anything you could be addicted to. I was living an up-close example of horrors of drug addiction and could see firsthand how addicts turned into monsters who could do unthinkable things to get that next hit.

There was a time he would show up in the middle of the night to my grandmother's house with dozens of large black nylon garbage bags. I would pretend to be asleep in bed, but I secretly watched with one eye open as he stuffed these heavy-looking bags into my bedroom closet. He would normally return a day or two later, at the same time, to pick up the bags.

One day, after he left, I tiptoed to the closet, quietly opened the door, and untied one of the bags. They were completely filled with rolled up wads of cash that were tied with a thick rubber band. Opening one of these bags released this intoxicating smell of money. The smell was addicting.

Life in Private School

During my sophomore year, my father sent me to one of the best private schools in Miami called Holy Cross Academy to play basketball since I didn't make the team at my local public school, Miami Senior High, which was always a powerhouse for basketball. That's where he and my mom played.

This private school was in an area of Miami I had never visited, the students were dropped off in fancy cars, and tuition costs were insane. But my father had money during this time. The money came from my those black bags in my closet.

My classmates were studying other languages like French and Latin; they wore blazers and ties as uniforms, but the most shocking was that they didn't put locks in their lockers. They didn't steal from each other which shocking to me. It felt exactly like Will Smith in the "The Fresh Prince of Bel-Air" except I didn't have a rich uncle Phil.

These kids were always talking about homework, prepping for SATS exams, and planning for university life. I had never heard of these universities and I had never seen so many people my age so interested in college and careers. I didn't understand why they were so stressed out about getting into a good university.

Things were starting to look up. School was hard, but I was learning so much. But being put into this environment did something to me.

Losing Hope

Growing up with few, if any, positive male role models, tired of being broke, and craving attention from my parents, I was disappointed by what I felt was my dark future. And as I compared my life to others, especially the rich kids in my private school, I honestly felt like nothing good was in store for my life.

I felt so inadequate. I was slowly losing hope. The more I focused on what was missing from my life—money, parents, stability, etc.—the darker my world became.

To make up for my insecurities I pretended to be something I wasn't. I kept a huge wad of the cash I had taken from my father's black bags in my pocket. The money inside the black bags was always perfectly wrapped in neat bundles and each wad had the same amount. I know this because one day I had the brilliant idea of taking some cash from one of the black bags.

It felt great walking around with cash in my pocket. I'd pull a huge wad of cash, in front of friends, to pay for stuff. Of course, the purpose of this spectacle was just to show off. Once, a friend from the basketball team asked where I got the money from and I said that I sold weed after school. He believed me.

At the time, I was using the money to help me make up for the insecurity I felt around such rich and successful kids.

There was so much money in those bags I never expected my father to notice. I was dead wrong!

He found out. My father never hit me, but I was terrified of him. He was quick tempered, and he just didn't seem like the type of person you want to get upset, so I confessed and made up a story of how I needed the money to pay for schoolbooks. I had a lot of difficulty with exams, but I could talk my way out of almost anything from being jumped, to not doing drugs, to getting away with terrible grades.

Despite the academic challenges, I was enjoying the new school and friendships. I was exposed to so much I had never seen or learned before. The irony in all of this is that the private school kids had more drugs than public school kids.

Then, at the end of my first year in my new school, I was called into a meeting with my math teacher, a nun. She explained I couldn't return the following school year because I was too far behind academically, especially in math, to catch up with my graduating class so they couldn't let me stay. I couldn't get over the fact that a nun, of all people, had kicked me out!

I was devastated, but the short time I spent there had really opened my eyes to a new world.

It's true; I was behind academically. But I also felt the administration didn't want me there. I'll never forget when the head priest had an issue of Time magazine, which had OJ Simpson's face on the cover. It was a controversial cover because OJ's face was darkened to make him look more menacing. The priest asked the entire class if I resembled OJ and from that day he would smile and call me "OJ" when he saw me.

Something about this guy disgusted me, but I didn't know what it was. During his talks, I daydreamed about all the ways I would take my revenge on him one day. The options were limitless. I thought about breaking a chair on his head or just punching him in his face. But I wanted to stay in this school more than I wanted to beat the crap out of him, so I put up with his taunts. Aside from violence, at this point in my life I wasn't sure how to deal with people like this.

During these years, I took comfort in stealing. I stole from anyone and not just my father. Stealing and shoplifting were like a sport for me. Sometimes I would make lists of stuff I wanted to take and could walk into a store and take it without being noticed. I was good, so I thought. I was such a scammer that sometimes I would switch the price tags on items to amounts I could afford. I'd walk up to the register, "pay for it," and be on the way without the alarms sounding.

One day without any prior planning, I walked into a Macy's department store with two friends, tried on a Polo sweater and sweatpants and used a five-finger discount (I took it) to pay. As I approached Macy's exit door the coast was clear. No security in sight. A few feet from the door one of my boys congratulated me on pulling it off. But as soon as I took my first step outside of the mall, several mall cops and police cars had a welcome reception for me.

It seemed as if I had just robbed a bank by the number of security and police involved in this massive operation.

In a matter of seconds, I was handcuffed, and rushed into the back seat of a police car. Sitting in the back of a police car for the first time was the most humiliating and humbling experience of my life, even to this day.

I'll never forget the police officer who arrested me. Instead of treating me like a thug or another statistic, he looked me straight in the eyes and told me I wasn't a criminal and that I didn't belong in jail. He told me to stay in school and stay off the streets. Since I was still a few months shy of being 18, I wouldn't be charged as an adult, so that was a huge relief for me.

I didn't realize it at the time, but during that short interaction, that cop was inviting me to live a new story. It was my choice to make. But you don't have to be arrested or go through experiences like this to choose a new story to live. Gradually, I started to realize we have the power and responsibility to choose the story we want to live. A story without limits or expectations set by others.

I also remember my father being constantly arrested for driving without a valid license and for unpaid parking tickets, but he was never arrested for anything more serious than that for some reason. He would often spend the night in jail and be released within a day or two, but never longer than that.

But he wasn't a free man.

There was a time that some gangster "bill collector" would come to collect my father's debts. When this guy looked at you it was clear that he was a straight up killer. When my father didn't have the money, the collector would show up at my grandmother's factory and tell her that if my father didn't come up with the money she might not see him again.

After the fire warning, she always reached into her purse and gave him whatever money she had. This went on for several months and it was terrifying for me. She seemed unusually calm though and composed during these situations.

Once my grandmother had to take an overnight bus to New York City frantically. She never left our neighborhood in Miami or took a vacation, so this was really strange. Eventually, I learned she needed to go because my father was being held for ransom because he apparently owed lots of money to someone. The kidnappers told my grandmother if she didn't pay, they were going to kill him.

I don't know how she did it, but she came up with the money to get him out of there, went to NYC on her own, and brought him back—

alive. One of the reasons why my grandmother never had any money was because most of it went to bailing out my father and my uncle from jail or to pay money they owed other people.

Once we were crossing an intersection when this car sped up and blocked us right in the middle of the road. Then this guy ran out of his car, opened my father's door and yelled, "Give me the truck or my money." He repeated this like 5 times so my father couldn't sneak a word in. I thought it was a carjacking at first until my father started negotiating with the man.

My father pointed at me and told the guy, "Don't do anything crazy I got my son in the car. I'll get you your money soon just give me some time." I couldn't believe it. The guy calmed down and he let us go WITH the car. But for a minute, I thought either my father was going to get shot or we'd be walking home.

That was life back then.

These situations were terrifying because it's not like I could have called the cops to ask for help. Those situations left me confused, disappointed, and angry about my father's chosen lifestyle because he was putting everyone in danger.

I felt worst of all for my grandmother because it seemed like what little money she had saved from her clothing business would also be spent covering my father's debts owed to his "business partners." At some point, I realized that my father and his brother preyed on my grandmother's unwavering love, generosity, and stubbornness to help them. She was an enabler.

I spent a lot of time telling her to stop bailing them out, but she just couldn't do it. Eventually, I came to peace with it and just let her be. My grandfather was present, but he didn't have a presence when it came to disciplining or leading the family.

My father wanted to have a "normal life." He experimented on multiple occasions with entrepreneurship, and he could have done well because he was using the same skill set (leadership, managing teams, and accounting) he used for the illicit stuff he was doing. But he couldn't break free from the story he believed about himself.

Maybe he felt he lacked the confidence, patience, or experience to succeed. As tough as he was, my father was unable to persevere through the ups and downs of starting a legal business and gradually developing it.

He was never addicted to drugs; well maybe weed because he always smelled like it. But his biggest addiction was fast money to support his lifestyle and image.

I also absolutely hated living on welfare, but I never blamed my father or resented him for that. Living on welfare felt like living under some bureaucratic social and psychological experiment. I felt so ashamed each time I had to pull out my wad of food stamps, which in those days looked like monopoly money, which made it obvious I was broke at the time of paying for food. I promised myself I would do everything possible so my future family would never live on welfare.

As a mental defense mechanism, I learned to embrace life on welfare to prevent other kids from making fun of me. Deep down, though, I felt humiliated, and I wanted us out of it. We tried so hard to get off welfare, but it felt like the system back then made it as difficult as possible to get out of it.

I don't know how the system works now, but back then if you opened a bank account and put money in it you'd be penalized and would either have your government assistance reduced or completely stopped before you were able to get back on your feet. It didn't make any sense to me.

Then during my second year in college, I'll never forget the morning when I heard a knock on the door. My uncle went to see who it was and found the sheriff standing there. The sheriff explained we had to vacate the property immediately because the bank had repossessed our home, but he would give us a few minutes to grab our most important belongings. Back then you weren't allowed to live in the house while the banks figured things out like today.

We were being foreclosed and I didn't even know we were behind on the mortgage payments. Actually, most of us didn't know. My grandmother had kept it to herself and was hoping it wouldn't come to this. She was too embarrassed to ask for help and had tried to deal with this on her own.

No one knew she had fallen behind on the mortgage payments, so this was completely unexpected. The sheriff, a tall African-American man, seemed short because he had his head hung low. He was visibly saddened for having to kick us out. It was clear from the expression on his face this wasn't something he enjoyed doing.

He looked sadder than us. And when he saw my cousin, Shannet sleeping in the baby crib, he nearly started crying but he composed himself. I was headed to the university to take some final exams. I quickly grabbed some photo albums, my best clothes, and whatever else I could fit into my beat-up two-door white Cadillac El Dorado (a gift from my father).

As we ran out, the sheriff sealed the door as we walked away from the home we knew after 10 years of living there. We never returned.

Forty-five minutes after stuffing my car full of my belongings, I drove to St. Thomas University, sat down in a quiet classroom, and took a final exam like nothing had happened. I don't remember what class it was, but I remember having a difficult time concentrating and thinking about where we were to going sleep. I could easily go to a friend's house, but what about my grandparent's, I thought to myself.

These experiences reinforced in me the desire to never be broke again. The instability, the never-ending money problems, and the drama affected me in so many ways. I didn't know what I would do in the future, but those experiences showed me where I didn't want to end up. At this point, I learned what I didn't want. And that's a start.

I wanted a different story, but I didn't know it at the time. I didn't realize it then, but all these experiences made me so disappointed, but at the same time, they were motivating me to look for something better. These experiences made me curious about why some people were successful, and others were not.

A little over a year later, my father passed away unexpectedly in a freak boating accident. He was fishing with two friends when the boat capsized at which point he hit his dead on the side of the boat, which caused a concussion. After that he couldn't swim and drowned according to the story we got from his friends with him that day who did survive. His autopsy also showed signs of cocaine in his system. Even though we weren't close and despite his lifestyle, I still loved him. After his death, I went through a short depression and had a hard time accepting this.

Then, about ten years later, my mother passed away too. She died due to a respiratory disease she developed after taking these weight loss pills called fen-phen. Within months of taking these weight loss pills, my mother started experiencing a shortness of breath and was easily tired. She stopped taking the pills after several months, but by that time it was too late. She had developed a condition that was terminal.

Within a few years, she didn't even have the energy to walk to the mailbox a few feet away, so she needed a wheelchair or golf cart to move around.

I had a closer relationship with my mother than I did with my father. I felt more comfortable talking to her, asking for her help, and just hanging out. At one point she asked me to live with her, but at that point I didn't feel like I needed a mother to look after me.

Near the end of my mother's life, she had a hole in her chest through which she had her medicine delivered. It was terrible watching her like this. It never occurred to me that some could lose both parents unexpectedly. I felt cursed at times.

A Better Story

After visiting 25 countries and living in eight of them, I have a very different perspective on the world from someone who has never traveled. I've seen miserable people in New York City and refugees in South Sudan thrilled to have a tent to sleep in. Perspective makes a huge difference.

I now choose to tell a better story and this allows me to see my obstacles as opportunities and consider my past 'disadvantages' as an asset. No tough or difficult experience should go to waste. Use it; don't let it use you. This decision has freed me to live a very different story from one I was telling myself in the past.

Regardless of where you come from, how much money you have, or where you live, everyone goes through their own sets of problems, struggles, or pain. The only difference is that some people choose to keep getting up after each fall.

You, too, can find your own advantageous perspective in life! There's nothing special about me. I'm not a psychologist, but I learned this through personal experience and not in a classroom. You can do it by finding nuggets of wisdom, principles, and lessons learned in your toughest experiences.

Let me show you.

I don't see myself as abandoned by parents. The best decision my parents made was in leaving me with my grandparents and never taking me back. What I lacked in material things, my grandmother made up for in love, discipline, and support. We never went on family vacations, I never got fancy gifts, and we never went to restaurants but I never went to bed hungry. There are so many people who have had it much worse than me. I had everything I needed.

My early experiences of being adopted, living in a factory, being arrested, and losing both parents early in life taught me to be grateful for every single thing in my life from a warm shower, to a bed, to my wife and kids. Those experiences have given me a new perspective on life; they've made me stronger, and they've taught me how to live in a constant state of gratitude. Without my rougher experiences, I'm not sure what type of father and husband I'd be today.

The shame and embarrassment of being arrested for shoplifting brought me a little closer to my father. As a consequence of my arrest, the judge ordered both of us to attend an obligatory counseling session. We also had to have a heart to heart talk, which we never really had. We didn't hug or kiss afterwards, but things were somehow a little different between us.

Another change I made after my arrest was to attend church with my maternal grandmother consistently. She took me to this church, which had this loud, and fiery Cuban-American pastor who was an incredible orator. His name was Pastor Delgado and he said things that helped inspire me to live a new story. One message, in particular, was like a seed that landed on fertile soil and stuck with me. He was speaking to the congregation, but it felt as if I was the only person in the church when he said something along the lines of, "you were born to sit at the table with kings and queens." That inspirational message and many others stayed with me.

Now I can say that I have been the guest of actual royalty, have met two U.S. Presidents, and have done some pretty cool things.

Use your perspective to overcome your circumstances. Looking back, I can see how everything that has happened has helped me become stronger. My pain is pushing me into purpose. Do I want to relive these events? No. But I'm not a victim either.

When you choose your story, you're actually taking responsibility for your life by changing your perspective. You're not an accident controlled by random events, so you don't have to live by chance. Choose your story, and you'll be on your way to being a Leader by Choice.

What Story Do You Want to Live?

You're not a hostage. Take your pen and have the courage to write the life you want to live. Reflect on the greatest version of your life's story you could possibly live and this will expand your options, your dreams, and your vision.

Your mind's creativity can work for you or against you. John Milton said, "The mind is its own place and in itself, can make a heaven of hell, a hell of heaven.

The mind works to fill in the gaps even when we don't know it's working. If you set a tough goal, your brain turns into a radar looking for anything that will help you achieve this goal. It's as if some type of internal GPS system in our brain has been activated and is trying to get you from point A to point B, whether you know it or not.

Your brain is always working, but if you don't give it a command (or a destination), it will go on autopilot and always look for the path of least resistance and most comfort. Be intentional about words and commands you give yourself. Your brain is always taking commands.

Remember the saying, "Sticks and stones can break my bones, but words can never hurt me"? The truth is words can do more damage than any stick or stone—if you don't take control of them. If you're constantly listening or repeating negative messages, those words will be the script your mind will follow. This is one of the reasons why I've intentionally cut passive cable-news watching, music with negative lyrics, and cursing.

One of my friends recently told me he has stopped saying, "I'm sorry," because this originated from the phrase "I'm a sorry individual." Instead, he says, "I apologize."

Pay attention to your words—they matter. When you change your words, you are pro-actively changing your story. And when you change your story, you change the focus of your thoughts, which changes your decisions, which changes your actions and your results.

Words matter.

Your story matters.

You matter.

Be Comfortable Being You

In 2016, I had the opportunity to spend a few minutes with President Obama during his trip to Cuba. He came to the U.S. Embassy in Havana, where I worked at the time and met the staff. He gave a short speech, shook hands with the employees, and took some pictures. One of the things I observed was how comfortable he was with himself. It seemed as if 'Obama the President' and 'Obama the man' were blended into one person. You could not separate one from the other. He knew who he was.

From my vantage point, it seemed like part of Obama's confidence comes from knowing who he is and being comfortable with himself—the good and the bad. Being comfortable with oneself is a theme I see repeated in the lives of so many leaders and not just Presidents. This has nothing to do with politics or political parties. I see it in all types of people regardless of their profession.

Being comfortable (or uncomfortable) with yourself is a choice. It took me a long time before I became comfortable in my own skin, but the process could have been faster if I had made a decision to believe in myself and knew that it's okay to fail, to make mistakes, and not be perfect. But eventually, I committed to become comfortable with myself regardless of what people thought about me.

Leaders don't pretend to be what they're not. They don't apologize for their core values (whether we agree or not). They don't have to be convinced about the value they bring to this world because they've convinced themselves already. Leaders see value in themselves first.

When it comes to having confidence in myself, one of the things that helped me is understanding that if people don't like me, it's not my problem; it's their problem. I don't have to be liked by everyone. It's an impossible and unhealthy goal to want to be liked by everyone. As long as my wife and kids love me, I can sleep just fine at night.

Your life, your voice, your opinion, your ideas, your soul, everything about you matters, but you have to value yourself, regardless of your circumstances, the size of your bank account, or how many followers you have on Instagram. Don't compare what you have to what others have been given.

Get Off Neutral

During my first posting as a United States Foreign Service Officer (diplomat), I was sent to Kigali, Rwanda. It was my first time in Africa. While there, I tried learning how to drive a manual (stick shift) car, but admittedly gave up after just the first lesson! It didn't help that I was learning to drive in a city full of hills. Whenever I stopped in traffic, I was on a hill, so I had a hard time of holding the brake and getting the car in neutral at the same time, so it just started rolling back down the hill!

A car in neutral can easily go forward or backward, depending on the slope where it's left. If you leave it on a hill and forget to put on the emergency brake, the car won't be there when you return. We can't treat our self-perception and self-worth like a car in neutral which moves on its own.

You're not a car on neutral; take control and decide you are a valuable person. Don't wait for someone else's appraisal, approval, or validation. Don't give anyone that power over you.

If you look in the mirror and don't love what you see, you're in big trouble. Learn to love yourself. Next time you look in the mirror blow a kiss yourself you-- sweet thang!

I'm not just talking about your physical looks. If you don't find a reason to love all of yourself and the person you're becoming, you're much more likely to allow your story to be written, told, and starred in by someone or something else. Don't roll down the hill of insecurity and hopelessness because your mind is set to neutral.

Get off neutral and decide who you are.

Stop waiting for others to accept you, choose you, or affirm you. Accept yourself first! If you wait for others to love and affirm you, it'll be like waiting for a buss that never comes. Love yourself first.

Are you waiting for a unicorn to tap you with their magical horn of instant happiness? Don't wait for the life of your dreams to start before you decide to be excited and happy now about where you are going. Start getting excited now about what you have and about what's coming. Aside from freaking people out, you'll eventually start excited. You can get now excited about the decisions you'll making and about the tiny steps forward you are going take.

Okay, so you're convinced. But how do you do this?

I have a confession to make.

I talk to myself—out loud. I really do. When I look in the mirror every morning, I say something like:

- I'm a leader, not a follower.
- I have integrity.
- I work hard.
- I'm a great husband and father.
- I'm blessed.
- Opportunities are coming my way.
- Today is a gift and I will make the most of it.
- I am always in the right place at the right time.
- God loves me and is working all things in my favor.

Using self-talk helps get my thinking off neutral and gives my brain intentional commands I set. I regularly give myself a pep talk because I can't depend on my boss, my wife, my kids, or someone on the street to encourage me. I choose to take responsibility for my emotions instead of leaving it up to chance, my feelings, or other people. Get out of neutral and decide how you want to feel and speak it into existence.

When motivational speaker Les Brown, a former radio DJ and politician, was in grade school, his teacher told him he had learning difficulties and he accepted it. He started living down to that description. When he explained to a new teacher he was diagnosed with a learning disability, the new teacher said, "Don't let the opinions of others become your reality."[5]

Les Brown didn't let someone else's words become his reality; instead, he chose his reality. You can decide your reality just as much as someone else can choose it for you. This doesn't mean you're ignoring your circumstances and real problems, but it means you're creating a reality based on hope, growth, and overcoming obstacles. You can create a reality where you don't accept excuses from yourself.

When you make a mistake, don't call yourself an idiot, a failure, or stupid. Just do everything possible to learn from your mistakes, understand why you made them, and move on. You're a human being and not a robot. Zig Ziglar said, "Remember failure is an event; not a person."[6]

You Always Lose When You Compare

When I was posted in Havana, Cuba my colleagues and I were invited to the set of Fast and the Furious 8, which was being filmed on the streets of Havana. While on the set, I got to see Vin Diesel from a distance. In person, he looks even taller, more muscular, and cooler than he does on camera. For a second, I was a little jealous.

I wish I had his voice, biceps, and famous friends laughing at my jokes. Then my life would be perfect! Not really, though because the comparing never stops. From my perspective, his life looks so appealing, but I have no idea what it's really like and what he's had to overcome to get where he is today.

If you spend a lot of time on Facebook or Instagram (should be called Insta-lie), you might feel like everyone has a life that's better than yours. We disproportionately share the good stuff about our lives, some of which are exaggerated and some are just made up, but as my wife said to me one day, "Everyone has some issue."

We can always find something about ourselves we don't like or that isn't perfect. One of the most important things I've done is stop comparing myself to others and start embracing and appreciating who I am, my experiences, and what I have to offer the world.

When we compare ourselves to others, we tend to focus on the things we don't have. And that's the problem with comparing. Comparing comes from a perspective where you can never win because it's based on partial information. When comparing we focus on the stuff that glitters, on the facade, and the superficial, while forgetting everyone has some issue. You will never have the complete picture when you compare yourself with someone else since you have no idea what others are going through behind closed doors.

Instead of comparing, remember that everything you're experiencing now is preparing you for the next level. There are things you have and can do that no one else can. When you see someone who is excelling, be happy for them, not envious. Your time is coming. But you can't do it if you are always wondering if your neighbor's grass is greener.

Here's the key: don't wait for your circumstances to change before you start enjoying and appreciating yourself and your unique life. Do it now before anything changes.

TIP: Don't check social media when you're feeling sad or right before going to bed. Nothing good can come from that.

Exercises

This section is designed to get you thinking about how the concepts in this chapter apply to your life. For each question, write as much or as little as you want without overthinking. Just write the first thing that comes to you. Download my free workbook from www.leaderbychoice.me/resources to write in your answers.

1. What is your old story?
2. What story have you accepted that is limiting your life?
3. What is your new story?

4. In what areas of your life have you been comparing yourself to others?

5. If your life was a message, what do you want it to be?

Chapter 2
CHOOSE TO KNOW THYSELF

"I freed a thousand slaves. I could have freed a thousand more if only they knew they were slaves." Harriet Tubman

A few days after arriving in Kigali, Rwanda for my first assignment I'll never forget when this baby-faced kid, who looked around 15 years old, rang my doorbell. He was wearing raggedy pants, a well-worn, faded t-shirt, and a friendly smile pasted on his face.

He told me his parents were killed in the Rwandan genocide, so I immediately felt sorry for him. He said he needed help paying for his school fees and explained the previous family who had lived in the house I had taken over was helping him. He explained his fees were about $20 per semester. I asked him a few questions to check if he was lying, but I knew I would give him the money.

I assumed he was a good kid and even though I had some suspicions, I helped him. After a few months of giving him money, one of my colleagues informed me this "kid" was actually an adult. He wasn't in school and he was using the money I gave him to buy drugs.

I felt so dumb!

This story reminds me that most of us have blind spots in our lives. Blind spots are those character traits, habits, or assumptions we normally make that can hurt us, but we don't see them. In my blind spot, I tend to be overly trusting of sob stories. I have a tendency to assume most people I meet have good intentions, but of course, that's not always the case. I like helping people who seem less fortunate without a second thought. Fortunately, my wife is better than I am at reading people. She's not as trusting as I am and this helps me balance out my blind spot.

In the end, a couple of security guards told this man-child to stop coming around, and I never saw him again. But if I hadn't been warned I might still be paying his "school fees" today.

Knowing yourself, or having self-awareness, means being aware of your blind spots, your personality traits, and your behavior—both good and bad—so you can manage yourself as well as possible. There are few things more important than knowing yourself. The goal of having self-awareness is not only to put yourself in situations where you know your strengths, weaknesses, and blind spots, but it's also used to help you master these things for your benefit.

Making mistakes like this is one of the ways you can learn about yourself, make adjustments, and continue moving forward. Study yourself, and you'll find blind spots. Then you'll be in a better position to make the most of who you are—managing your weaknesses and enhancing your strengths.

There's a quote associated with Charles Darwin, which says, "It is not the strongest of the species that survives, nor the most intelligent that survives. It is the one that is most adaptable to change."[7] The people who learn continuously stay relevant and are best prepared to change for the better. Without changing we die.

The way this applies to life is that it doesn't matter where you begin, instead what matters is where you're headed. If you learn from your mistakes and allow them to become opportunities for increased self-awareness and growth, you'll soon find you're in a cycle of continuous learning.

Basically, if there's something you want to improve in your life, developing the ability to assess yourself can help you determine your next steps. Self-awareness doesn't show you how to get from point A to point B, but it does show you the potential roadblocks along your journey. When you can seek feedback, listen actively, and use personality profiles to study yourself, you will be on your way to cultivating a mindset, which embraces self-awareness and personal honesty.

What Blind Spots Do You Have?

I was watching one of those home makeover shows once, and I'll never forget this episode where a guy we'll call Mark, only because I forgot his name, was selling his home because he was getting divorced. During the tour of Mark's home, the host of the show kept finding unfinished DIY projects throughout the house, like incomplete paint jobs, burnt out light bulbs, and unfinished carpentry work. These were all projects that Mark's wife had asked him to do, but for some reason he never completed them.

By the time they finished the tour, they had found around 10 minor jobs he left unfinished. When they asked Mark about all the unfinished projects, he casually explained he didn't have time to finish them. I can't prove this, but I suspect there's a connection between Mark's divorce and these unfinished projects. If Mark wasn't taking these responsibilities seriously, then what else did he leave undone? It seems like Mark wasn't able to see the impact this blind spot had on other parts of his life. But listening to constructive feedback or criticism is hard, so I'm not going to pretend otherwise. However, those moments are pure gold, for those who listen, because of the things we can learn from them. Most people prefer listening to useless compliments rather than to difficult life-changing truths.

I've been married now for 10 years to someone who is, thankfully, the complete opposite of me in many areas. It's frustrating at times being married to someone who is strong where I'm weak, but it's also a blessing because together, we can achieve more than if we were separate. There's a secret advantage to being married or having people around you who are willing to speak the truth to you. But it takes courage to listen and put your ego aside: that's what self-leadership looks like.

Are there areas in your life where you are repeatedly not meeting expectations?

Are there supervisors or colleagues who have given you honest feedback about areas where you need improvement but you haven't listened?

Look for opportunities to get feedback and shine a light on your blind spots instead of keeping them in the dark.

Why Is Self-Awareness Important?

When American Idol first started, everyone wondered how it was possible that people who sang so badly didn't know it. At first, it was hard to believe there are people who are so clueless about their musical abilities. I thought the show was fake. Not only could some of these contestants not sing, but some also believed they were the next Alicia Keys.

How does this happen?

Sometimes it happens because the people around them are not being honest. Other times it's because some people don't want to listen to the feedback they've been given. If you don't recognize having had a problem or weakness, you won't do something about it.

If I had known more about my blind spot concerning sob stories, I could have asked a few friends first if they knew anything about this kid who was asking me for money. If Mark had known he was prone to leaving projects unfinished or what impact this was having on his wife, he might have considered asking for help or paying someone to finish the work. There should be some signs or a history of problems if you look closely under the microscope.

I've heard some people say we should completely ignore our weaknesses. That approach might work for some, but not for most. If I completely ignored my weaknesses, my life would be a mess. I wouldn't be able to learn new skills, take new risks, or stick with something that's difficult, like writing this book, starting a business, or working to become a better husband. Self-awareness can help you see that difficulty doesn't necessarily mean it's a weakness. The goal is to recognize your weaknesses, so you can manage and not ignore them.

Before deciding to ignore your weaknesses completely, it's important first to understand the difference between a true weakness and an opportunity for improvement.

Writing has never been my strength or passion, but I choose to see it as an opportunity or a challenge. Writing is a skill I want to develop because it helps me exploit my deep interests in public speaking, authoring, and coaching. Writing is something I need to manage and not master. I've gotten to this point by self-assessing my strengths, weaknesses, and my opportunities for improvement, but I had to be real with myself, and you do too.

Being honest with yourself and having the courage to self-assess is the key to putting yourself on a positive cycle of understanding who you really are and what adjustments you have to make to take life to the next level. There's nothing wrong with you, and I'm not trying to change you, but all of us have room for improvement.

If you want to remain where you are, then all you have to do is keep doing the same things. But if you want to become a Leader by Choice or if you want to see and experience new achievements, which is why you picked up this book, and are investing your time in reading it, then it will require gradual, but constant self-improvement.

My business coach, Kendall Flicklin, says, "Each next level of your life is going to require a different you." Think of this process as a marathon and not as a sprint. Continue building on your strengths and managing your weaknesses to continually create new versions of yourself for each level of your life.

What a First-Grade Spelling Test Taught Me About Focus

One day, my daughter, who was in first grade at the time, said she got one question wrong on a spelling test. Being the great parents that my wife and I are, we zeroed in on the one word she misspelled. Instead of starting off by praising her for the nine she got right, we grilled her about the one she missed. Even though she said she tried her best, we weren't convinced with her explanation.

The following week at a parent-teacher conference, my daughter's teacher said, "Your daughter always tries her best, helps others, and works hard at everything she does. When she says she tried her best, you should know she really does try her best." When she said that, I felt awful! After our discussion, do you think it mattered to me she misspelled one word? Not at all.

(By the way I'm not a perfect parent, so stop judging me. I can feel it!)

This experience taught me that at times we tend to spend too much time and energy on the wrong things. We end up focusing solely on what we did wrong and forget about all the things that are going well. Sometimes, we disproportionately focus on life's distractions, what we lack, our mistakes, and our weaknesses.

We live in a culture obsessed with improving weaknesses in awful detail, but that's not where the majority of our time and energy has to go. Like management guru Peter Drucker says, "It is much more difficult to be proficient at your weaknesses than it is to become excellent at your strengths."[8] Operating from your strengths energizes you.

Like regulating the thermostat on an air conditioning unit to get the best temperature, we want to control our strengths and weaknesses so we know how best to exploit them instead of just obsessing about our weaknesses or only relying on our strengths.

The Greatest Award in Sports

"And the award for the 1996 Most Valuable Player on the boys' basketball team goes to—Aramis." My insecure and fragile high school ego was destroyed. I should have won the MVP that year. I was robbed! Instead, I took home something called the "Coach's Award," which meant absolutely nothing for my high school ego. I've never even heard of a coach's award!

Sports fans primarily focus on the Most Valuable Player (MVP) award every year. Like most fans, I had always believed it's the most important award, but that changed when I read Growing Up Gronk: A Family's Story of Raising Champions. The book tells the story of the Gronkowski family and how two parents unintentionally created a sports dynasty with their five sons.

At the time the book was written, four out of the five brothers from this family had played professional sports. One played professional baseball, and three played in the NFL at the same time. And the youngest of the five boys, who was in college at the time, was expected to be the most gifted athlete in the family.

The story focuses a lot on the family's mindset, training, parenting, exercise habits, and above all, determination, which caused these boys to compete at the highest levels. The author deconstructed the family's success to see what other families could replicate. If I could boil down this family's success down to one thing, it would be their mindset.

The story that best captures the importance of their mindset is when one of the brothers proudly described having won multiple Most Improved Player awards in the NFL. To me, the Most Improved Player sounds even worse than my Coach's Award, but it's one of the most important awards an athlete can receive, because it signifies continuous learning, adapting, and improving.

What makes great athletes great is their dissatisfaction with their current level of performance. Winning an MVP means you reached the top. But it's the athletes who are intentionally looking for ways to improve their game who get better. Practicing alone doesn't make you better. They might not win the MVP, but by focusing on improving, they are taking responsibility for something they can control—a mindset of continuous improvement.

Focusing on the MVP award is elusive, but focusing on small daily improvement is straightforward and measurable.

The reason athletes like Michael Jordan and Kobe Bryant won so many MVPs throughout their careers wasn't because they were the most gifted or athletic. It was because they were constantly looking for ways of adapting their shots and skills to compete against athletes who were focused on stopping them. They won so many MVPs because they developed a growth mindset that was focused on constant improvement.

Focusing on tiny improvements is tangible because we can identify those opportunities for getting better, but you have to know yourself first; you need self-awareness. This all ties in with you being a Leader by Choice because you have to have the ability to self-assess and identify those areas in your life where you can improve.

What Do You Really Really Really Want?

I saw a documentary about Beyoncé once and the part that stood out to me the most was during her time of struggle. There was a time in her career when she felt lost or like something was missing. She was frustrated with her life and the direction her career was going. At that point, she asked herself one question:

"What do I really want?"

When she was finally able to answer that question, she took her personal and professional life in a new direction and found personal contentment that was not based on what others defined as success and happiness.

For mere mortals like you and I, we should take time to stop and think about what we really want out of life and where we're headed too. Just like Beyoncé, we need to know what we are working towards and understand why our current situation might not be working. If you're going through some frustrating circumstances, but you don't know what's causing it, it's really easy to get distracted from what really matters. Instead, though, seek to understand yourself and what you want, and then decide how to get there.

There was a time when I was really frustrated in my career. All I knew was I didn't like my job, but I wasn't clear on why or what I really wanted and this was affecting me in a lot of ways. I would come home feeling mentally exhausted, so I wouldn't have any energy to play with my kids or help them with their homework or talk to my wife. I thought all I needed was a new career.

But the truth is I didn't know what I liked or disliked about my career. I had to take the time to journal, read about purpose, careers, and vocations, work with a career coach, and self-assess to clarify what I was running from and more importantly where I wanted to go. Am I currently in my dream job? No. But I realized that just finding a new job wasn't the answer to my problems.

I feel 100% better even though I'm still in the same career. How, you might ask? Because I know what I want and I know where I'm going. And I'm taking tiny, consistent action towards my vocational dreams step by step, and that feels awesome. I no longer have this pressure on me to quit my career or to find something else to do.

I've done this by focusing on making an impact or bringing value where I am. And because of that, I don't feel stuck or under someone else's control because I'm taking daily consistent action, even if I'm just doing one small thing per day at least I know I'm actively working toward my dreams. Plus, making an impact where I am has shown me the importance of bringing value to wherever I am regardless of my title or profession. You can learn more about yourself from being a person of value than being someone who is only thinking about getting out.

The key for me was clarifying the type of career, marriage, children, and future I wanted. Running away from pain is not enough. When you get clear on the life you want it changes everything because you now have a target to aim at. When you know where you're going, it's much easier to see the steps you need to take, and it's also easier to stay locked to a target. Self-awareness is important for not only knowing what's causing your pain but for understanding what makes you fulfilled.

If you're not clear on what you really want from your life, I have some questions for reflection at the end of the chapter. Take a few minutes to write them down. Don't just think about them—write out your thoughts and responses. When you physically write something down, the words and ideas expressed are different than when you simply think about it in your head.

Are You Fighting the Resistance?

I was watching an animated movie with my kids called The Croons. It's about a family living during the Stone Age. The main character, Grug, was responsible for keeping his family safe. For him, that meant keeping everyone in the cave, away from dangerous animals, experiences, and the unknown, which he was taught only leads to death. He constantly retold his family a story about the tragic consequences of leaving the cave.

The family would only leave to hunt and always stayed close by, until one day when his teenage daughter saw a firefly for the first time and started chasing it. She was so amazed by its color that she followed it outside of the cave, which led her to see surrounding areas she'd never seen. When she returned from her adventure, she ran into her angry father. In the argument that followed, the father explained it was his job to keep the family alive, which meant keeping everyone in the cave. And in a moment of self-awareness, the daughter said, "Living in a cage is not really living."

Some of us are living in a self-imposed cage, but we don't know it because we don't have any self-awareness. Self-awareness can open our eyes and reveal if we're unwilling to leave the cave, which represents our comfort zone. Avoiding new experiences because of the fear of embarrassment, failure, or uncertainty is stale living. Yes, it's safe and comfortable, but what else can you expect?

One of the tricky things about life is that we can become so wrapped up in our daily routines and problems that we fool ourselves into thinking that we're really living, but we're only halfway there. If we don't venture outside the cave, we'll miss out on so much more adventure, new experiences, and the heart of who you really are and what you can do.

One of the biggest risks in life is only pursuing comfort and safety at all times. While the cave protects us from embarrassment or failure, or both, personal growth only comes from situations where we are challenged or stretched. Staying in the cave was critical when predators were stalking us for dinner. But now staying in the cave is a liability.

Self-awareness is also a tool which helps us understand what is holding us back from making positive changes in life or taking action towards something greater. Self-awareness helps us see that a lot of what we say is holding us back are nothing more than excuses.

This thing holding us back has a name. Some people call it resistance, fear, hesitation, etc. No matter what you call it, it's a real thing. And that's the enemy.

The resistance has one job—to keep you, your dreams, and your greatest life in the cave away from personal significance. The craziest thing about the resistance is that it grows as we get closer to stepping outside of the cave. It's your job to recognize it and act on it.

I love how entrepreneur and author Seth Godin describes this topic:

"The resistance is the voice in the back of our head telling us to back off, be careful, go slow, compromise. The resistance is writer's block and putting jitters and every project that ever shipped late because people couldn't stay on the same page long enough to get something out the door."[9]

The first step in getting out of the cave is understanding when you're in it. Once you know where your boundaries are, you know where you have to go. You can see these boundaries as walls holding you back, or as a starting point for growth. Writing this book has been a daily fight against the resistance's quiet whispers in my ear telling me not to publish this book because of the possible embarrassment I might face if no one reads it, or worse if people criticize it.

With all that said, we still need the cave for rest, sleep, relaxation, safety, and security. We can't be way outside our comfort zone all the time and we shouldn't try, so the key here is to find a healthy balance between risk and comfort. Before I wrote this book, I blogged for about two years. Blogging, at first, was way outside my comfort zone, but the more I did it, the less intimidating it became. But blogging gave me some experience and confidence, which I used in writing this book.

Look for tiny steps that can give you a chance to test and push the boundaries of your comfort zone. You don't have to bungee jump or try other extreme sports to push your limits. Instead, take baby steps toward the entrance of the cave and eventually take one tiny step out into the light. Then take another step and then another one. You don't have to jump.

What Makes You Come Alive?

The thing I love doing the most is public speaking, but not just any speaking. I love sharing inspirational stories that help people connect the dots in their lives so they can think differently, have a new perspective, or try achieving things they didn't think was possible. But I didn't know I loved public speaking initially. In fact, during my first speech in college, I completely bombed! My college professor said he didn't understand what I said.

However, over time, I realized that I loved it, so I kept trying and in the process started getting better. But this process of discovery wasn't quick or automatic.

It took some time to find out what makes me come alive. And I had to test it often to see if it's true. This is why I really believe all of us have something that makes us come alive, but for most people, it takes time to find it and make that connection. The problem is most people quit or aren't willing to stick with something long enough to see themselves get and develop a for it.

If you don't know what that thing is for you, developing your self-awareness can help you find it. Have you ever noticed there are people who are really good at certain things, but they don't even know it? You might be like that too. Some people fall into this category because the thing they do really well comes naturally to them, so they underestimate it. You might have an undiscovered superpower you're not even aware of.

Imagine for a minute just how exciting your life would be if you found something that made you jump out of bed in the morning—without an alarm clock. Wouldn't that be a great feeling? Well, I still need an alarm clock because I'm waking up at 5:00, but I wake up excited because I feel like I'm on a mission; I'm working on something exciting, risky, and fun because there's some potential there for something awesome to come from it.

You can choose a mission too—one that's exciting and interesting enough for you to jump out of bed for. We'll talk more about your mission later.

In the book Wild at Heart, John Eldredge shares a story of how one day he was in a bookstore, randomly flipping through the pages of a book. He read a quote so powerful he immediately closed the book, put it back on the shelf, and ran home because it changed him completely. The quote comes from Howard Thurman, a theologian, and clergyman and it reads, "Don't ask what the world needs. Ask what makes you come alive and do it. Because what the world needs is people who have come alive."[10]

Understanding what makes you come alive is one of the greatest things that will happen in your life after investing time in knowing yourself. But I have to warn you that it won't be easy or quick for most people so learn to enjoy the process. Everything you experience on this journey of self-discovery is there to help and prepare you for the next level. It's like a video game. The levels get incrementally harder, but as you master one before moving on to the next, you become better prepared to face the more difficult challenges coming your way.

Sometimes, what makes you come alive is that thing you've been thinking about, but have not tried because of fear and resistance. Step out of the cave to find out. Or it might be something you need to do more of to gain mastery. The point is that it takes self-discovery and time to understand yourself. Don't get upset or disappointed if you're in the dark because it's taking longer than you thought.

Lose your expectations and just keep taking action, experimenting, and testing, and you will get there. When you feel most lost is actually when you're getting closest to understanding.

In fact, I think most people have no clue what makes them come alive. They don't have a mission or something they can devote themselves to. They either don't know it or are so distracted by shiny objects they've ignored their calling or the things that really make them come alive. What's even worse is when someone has given up the search. Finding the thing(s) that makes you come alive is a choice, but it requires commitment.

This is your race, so run it without looking to the sides. You're not competing against anyone else, and you don't have to worry about whether the thing that makes you come alive makes sense to anyone else. It's your thing; made just for you. Where you start the race of life doesn't matter. What's important is where you're headed.

Think of it as your personal and intimate gift to you from God, the universe, unicorns or whatever the heck you believe in. Others won't understand it so don't get upset when they don't care or when they don't support you. It's for you, not them. Develop the self-awareness to learn what excites you, sparks your curiosity, or pisses you off like nothing else.

Understanding what makes you come alive will give you the vision and inspiration you need to move forward because you can't just focus on the things you don't like. While those are important things to know, they are just half of the puzzle. You need both determination and direction, as Angela Duckworth says in her book Grit: The Power of Passion and Perseverance.

Okay, so you're convinced, but how can you develop your self-awareness? Let's keep it real; it's not easy and it's something that never stops. Benjamin Franklin explained it best when he said, "There are three things that are extremely hard: steel, a diamond, and to know one's self."[11] But you can improve with practice, because it's just like any other skill, and all skills can be improved.

Developing Your Self-Awareness

There are three things we can do to gain more self-awareness or clarity as to who we are and what we want: WAR—Write, Ask, and Read.

Write

I used to think keeping a journal was for kids, but it actually feels great to dump your thoughts, frustrations, and ideas on paper (or computer). Sexy beasts like us have a lot of stuff in our heads, and we need to get them out to clear our minds. This process of mental dumping helps relieve stress, maintain a healthy perspective, and get anxiety in check.

Extracting your thoughts is like letting a little air out of a balloon that's about to pop. Writing and journaling is also a great way of keeping a record of your personal growth, tracking and exploring your blind spots, and collecting clues about what makes you come alive. It's also a great tool for stress release for people like me who have a hard time expressing their feelings.

In this super-connected, always-looking-at-a-screen world, we desperately need time to stop, turn off distractions, and think! In Essentialism, by Greg McKeown, he beautifully explains, "Clarity of purpose allows us to succeed at greater levels." This type of clarity comes from introspection or self-analysis. It takes time to investigate our dreams, desires, and goals, and by writing we can journal our way to having more clarity. Journaling doesn't have to take a lot of your time. You can write one sentence or one page.

Another effective way of getting your thoughts out of your head is through blogging. Blogging has been one of the best things I've done to help me gain clarity into which things I really care about like leadership, mindset, and personal development. One of the benefits of blogging is that you can share your ideas, passions, frustrations, and dreams with others and in the process connect with like-minded people. Blogging can help you narrow down the core issues or topics you enjoy discussing.

RESOURCE: If you are interested in joining a group of new bloggers, check out the Live Your Legend community.[12]

If you have never blogged, this might sound a little scary (or exciting). You might think you don't have anything to blog about, but that's not true. The greatest secret in blogging is this—but don't tell anyone—just start. Don't worry about what to write about and just write about the journey. Your first posts will be terrible, and that's how they should be. The more you write, the more clarity you'll get about your next post.

Ask

When my kids were two years old, they each passed through a "why" stage. No matter what I said or how detailed an explanation I gave, they responded with "Why?" Sometimes, I would answer about four or five "why" questions in a row, which drove me crazy, but each time I answered, we went deeper into the heart of the matter.

As adults, most of us don't ask why anymore. Maybe it's because we assume we know everything already. Wouldn't it be great if we had the same attitude of wonder and curiosity as children? We need to go deeper to understand ourselves, our desires, and the things that make us come alive and we can do this by asking ourselves, "Why?" For example, whenever you repeat the same mistake, or you avoid something you should do or when you experience something you really enjoy, ask yourself why.

Another way of increasing self-awareness is by asking the people close to you, like your spouse, best friends, boss or colleagues, what they think about you. At work, you can ask your boss for honest feedback about your opportunities for improvement, but the key to doing this is not to be offended when people are completely honest with you. Give them the freedom to speak frankly.

For example, if you are married or have a close friendship, you can ask that person what areas in your life could be improved. Yes, I know it seems shallow and strange to talk about yourself, but once you try it, you'll be surprised by the feedback. Sometimes other people can see things in you that you can't see in yourself.

Read

Looking at your bookshelf can say a lot about you and your interests, and this is huge. When I decided where to focus for my long-term vocational goals, one of the things I did was think about the books I enjoyed reading most. It turns out they were mostly about leadership and personal development. Looking at what you're already interested in can show you something about yourself you never really noticed before.

There are so many books written just to help people gain more self-awareness about themselves, their strengths, and their greatest purpose. There are so many I enjoyed, but these are the three best that I've read:

1. Man's Search for Meaning by Victor Frankl
2. Managing Oneself by Peter F. Drucker
3. Unique Ability by Catherine Nomura and Julia Waller

Another hack for gaining tremendous amounts of self-awareness is by taking personality assessments. There are too many to list here, and I'm not an expert, but I've taken a bunch of them, and I found a few of them to be really insightful.

I'm sure you've heard about the Myers-Briggs Type Indicator, but there are other assessments. These two assessments aren't free, but they're the ones I've learned the most from.

1. DISC personality profile
2. Strengths Finder 2.0

These two assessments have helped me save time by speeding up the process of connecting the dots of my strengths and the type of work I'll enjoy the most. Often, I find out something I never realized, but I can see is true about myself or I'll learn how to compensate for weakness.

I recommend you take the DISC first, study it for a few weeks, and then take the Strengths Finder 2.0. You can find links to these personality profiles on the resources page of my website.

Continually exploring and knowing yourself is a necessary tool in helping you identify your strengths, opportunities for improvement, what makes you come alive, and, most importantly, your attitude. If you don't know what makes you happy, sad, or inspired, you won't know the best choices to make when opportunities come your way. Is this the only way it can be done? No. But knowing thyself will definitely increase your chances of being a Leader by Choice because you'll be able to choose the right adjustments to make at the right time.

Exercises

The goal of these exercises is to better understand your "default" behavior, your likes and dislikes, and your attitude. Remember, there's nothing wrong with you, but the more you learn about yourself, the more opportunities you'll find to make the right adjustments.

1. On a scale from 1 to 10, how do you rate your default behavior? (1 being super nice and 10 being a super jerk)

   1 2 3 4 5 6 7 8 9 10

2. How do you rate your default behavior? (1 being a pushover and 10 being a dictator)

   1 2 3 4 5 6 7 8 9 10

3. How do you rate your default behavior? (1 being you keep your opinion to yourself and 10 being you seek to impose your opinion)

   1 2 3 4 5 6 7 8 9 10

4. How good of a listener are you? (1 being a non-stop talker and 10 a constant listener)

   1 2 3 4 5 6 7 8 9 10

5. How well do you know your strengths and weaknesses? (1 being zero awareness and 10 I know exactly)

   1 2 3 4 5 6 7 8 9 10

6. How confident are you? (1 being most of your time is spent doing stuff you dislike and 10 being all of your time is spent doing things you love)

   1 2 3 4 5 6 7 8 9 10

7. How connected do you feel with something greater than you? (1 being not connected at all and 10 being fully connected)

   1 2 3 4 5 6 7 8 9 10

8. How much effort are you putting into creating the life you really want? (1 being no effort and 10 being maximum effort)

   1 2 3 4 5 6 7 8 9 10

9. How valuable do you consider yourself? (1 being worthless and 10 being extremely valuable)

   1 2 3 4 5 6 7 8 9 10

10. When someone gives you constructive feedback, how likely are you to listen and apply it? (1 being you never listen and 10 being you always listen actively)

    1 2 3 4 5 6 7 8 9 10

11. How do you define a successful life?

12. What activity (or activities) have you participated in that made you feel the most alive?

Chapter 3
CHOOSE YOUR ATTITUDE

"Your attitude, not your aptitude, will determine your altitude." Zig
Ziglar

Once I worked with someone who was constantly in some trouble at
work due to simple mistakes, rude behavior, or not meeting basic
expectations. Whenever someone tried to counsel this employee, it
was never his fault. He always had an explanation on why the
problem wasn't his fault. My colleague had an attitude problem that
came from an inability or unwillingness to listen, accept
responsibility, and make improvements.

After studying and learning about so many successful and not so
successful people through biographies and personal experiences, I
can say without any hesitation that attitude is the most powerful
indicator of success I know. It's not connections, money, or
education.

Nothing in this book can help if you have the wrong attitude.

As a manager, I have interviewed approximately 200 people over the past 10 years. Do you know what I'm primarily looking for? Attitude. I'm looking for a window that offers a glimpse of the applicant's real attitude. Most of the questions I ask aren't just about their education, experience, or skills. I'm looking for clues that reveal who they are and what their attitude will be like weeks, months, and possibly years into the job.

It's almost impossible to work with someone who has a bad attitude, no matter how skilled they are. A person with poor skills and the right attitude can be trained to do anything, but a person with a bad attitude and great skills is an energy and time vampire.

Attitude is an inner quality that converts your failures into learning opportunities and teaches you to love doing what most people hate. Attitude is similar to an invisible quality that determines how you choose to respond to the external stimuli called—life! The problem is most people didn't know they were born with this superpower because it's disguised as a skill. Like any other skill, your attitude can be developed.

I wish someone had told me years ago I had the ability to choose my attitude. Maybe someone did try to teach me, but I wasn't ready to listen because I didn't have the right attitude.

Despite our experiences, we have the ability and the responsibility to choose our attitude. If you don't believe me, I hope to convince you that, regardless of what you're going through, you were created in such a magnificent way that the freedom to choose your attitude remains with you at all times despite your circumstances, setbacks, and number of Instagram followers.

Before moving on to other core decisions, it's crucial that you internalize this philosophy on attitude. If you have the right attitude, no setback will keep you down for too long. There are people with terrible attitudes, but they don't even know it, like my colleague. While self-awareness is crucial for understanding who you are, the attitude with which you choose to confront the world is what will determine your future success. Self-awareness helps you understand if your attitude is helping or hurting you. You can't have long-term success with a short-term mindset.

Who Really Controls Your Attitude?

Victor Frankl was a survivor of three different Nazi death camps. In 1942, Frankl's father, mother, brother, and wife were arrested in Vienna and taken to concentration camps. They were separated, and so they lost contact. Eventually, Frankl would come to learn that the only family member to survive the camps was his sister. The others died without him knowing when or how. While in the camps for three years, Frankl, a psychiatrist by training, vividly described the

76

horrors of everyday life, but those experiences gave him a first-hand account of the power of attitude in the worst of times.

Frankl's book, Man's Search for Meaning, gives us a thorough sense of the horror of life in concentration camps. Not only were the Jewish prisoners literally worked and tortured to death, but they were also put through psychological torture. Prisoners never knew when it was going to be their turn to be sent to the gas chamber or stand in front of a firing squad, so they lived in constant fear of death and in the most inhumane conditions. But from Frankl's writing, we are shown a pattern of which prisoners would die first.

The first Jews to die were those who weren't strong enough to perform the grueling daily work. Frankl hypothesized that the prisoners who did not have something to live for were the ones who lost hope first. And the ones who lost hope started to die internally through a negative shift in their attitude. According to Frankl, prisoners who felt they had nothing or no one to live for had given up on life first, so they appeared to be in the worst physical condition, so they were the first ones to be put to death.

So, what kept Frankl going?

Throughout his experience, the thought of reuniting with his loving wife and family kept him motivated. They were separated upon entering the camp, so he didn't know anything about their safety, but the possibility of being reunited filled him with hope and meaning.

He was also motivated to rewrite a psychology book he was working on that he had lost when he entered the camp. Using scraps of paper and working in dark secluded areas, Frankl was hard at work completing this book, and it became his life's work while in the camps.

Like other prisoners who seemed to be doing better than others, Frankl had intentionally chosen something to live for. This decision changed his attitude, which gave him hope and helped him survive.

Frankl teaches us that when people choose something or someone to live for it gives them hope, purpose, and meaning. And this hope will give them a reason to keep going. Some people call this their "why." In other words, when you choose something to live for, it will keep you going in the midst of the most difficult circumstances. In Man's Search for Meaning, Frankl explains, "Everything can be taken from a man but one thing: the last of the human freedoms—to choose one's attitude in any given set of circumstances; to choose one's own way."

Thankfully, most of us will never experience life in a concentration camp, but through Frankl, we can learn that we have the ability to choose our attitude by deciding how we respond to our circumstances and where we look for hope and meaning. Frankl also clarifies that "Between stimulus and response, there is a space. In that space is our power to choose our response. In our response lies our growth and our freedom." A man who lived in a concentration camp for three years shows us that regardless of our physical confinement, obstacles, or struggles, the one thing that can never be taken is our ability to choose your attitude.

If Victor Frankl was able to find something to live for in the midst of so much death, then what about you?

Focus on Hope

I love my grandmother with all my heart, but every time I call her she wants to give me a detailed report on the latest criminal news reports on murders, home invasions, and rapes. I always tell her I'm not interested in talking about the news to which she calls me irresponsible for not staying up to date. She usually ends the phone call, with a "Please be careful out there."

I'm not interested in the latest news or horror stories because it doesn't do me any good. Instead, I read for anything that's particularly important and then move on. If you spend your evenings glued to the news, like my grandmother, your worldview (attitude) will most definitely be impacted by the daily reports of crime, murder, and mayhem. To capture as much attention as possible, the news is a combination of entertainment, sensationalism, and celebrity breakups sprinkled with bits of fear to keep us coming back for more, but the majority of that information is useless for consumers, but good for profits.

Sure, discrimination, poverty, and war still exist throughout the world. But overall things are getting better when you compare how we live today with the world just 30, 20, or even 10 years ago. There have been improvements in the most important key areas like education, health, nutrition, and standards of living. I read something in Reader's Digest that caught my attention.

"The rich get richer, but the poor do even better. Between 1980 and 2000, the poor doubled their consumption. The Chinese are 10 times richer and live about 25 years longer than they did 50 years ago. Nigerians are twice as rich and live nine more years. The percentage of the world's people living in absolute poverty has dropped by over half. The United Nations estimates that poverty was reduced more in the past 50 years than in the previous 500."[13]

But as things get better, we're much more likely to be bothered by things that are not going well even if really small. That's not the perspective I choose to have. I could have as easily found an article about how this world is being destroyed, but how will that help anyone? Focusing on the negative will not help me do something positive. Instead, I choose to live with hope instead of fear. And hope encourages me to take positive action.

What we consume matters, because like food, what comes in must go out. If you feast on a steady diet of negative media and people, what type of impact will this have on your attitude, and the decisions you make? I've noticed that phenomenal people follow an extreme diet of carefully curated (almost zero) negative entertainment, news, and unintentional social media usage. The good news is that the change you want to see in the world starts with your attitude.

Your Perspective Matters

A few years ago, I was traveling with my wife and our three daughters, who were between six months and four years old at the time. You know that family in the plane with the crying baby, one kid running around, and one having a breakdown on the floor? Yeah, that was us. I had a stroller in one hand and a baby in the other, and was somehow pushing a luggage cart overflowing with suitcases.

We were a hot mess and completely exhausted!

I was not sure if we could make our next flight, but I wanted to stop by the airline's main desk to ask the clerk if she could check if our seats were together. With a pathetic "my-life-is-so-hard" look on my face, I said to the customer service agent, "I have a problem. I'm traveling with my wife and my three kids and..." but before I could finish the sentence, she looked at me dead straight in the eyes and with a super serious face said:

"Congratulations."

She interrupted my pity party to congratulate me! She completely ignored my exhaustion and circumstances. That word "congratulations" was loaded with meaning. She completely changed my attitude with just one word. What she was saying was congratulations for being so privileged and financially blessed that you're able to travel internationally with such a beautiful and healthy family. In other words, she reminded me that I had nothing to complain about.

Thinking about my situation from her perspective completely changed my attitude with one word. Without saying it, she made me realize just how fortunate I was.

This experience showed me that attitude is based on our perspective and not our circumstances.

Excusitis

Excusitis is a national epidemic. It's a psychological disease preventing people from having a vision, accomplishing goals, and taking action because of fictitious mental obstacles.

If you're reading this book, I can make some general assumptions about you:

1) You have a sound mind.
2) You're probably not homeless.
3) You have some disposable income.
4) You have some disposable time.
5) You can find answers to problems.

No one but you is responsible for your goals, dreams, and aspirations. And no one but you is responsible for the decisions you choose to make. It's your responsibility, and no one has the power to give it or take it away from you.

Just ask yourself one thing.

Is there someone in your same situation, or worse, who is still attacking life and pursuing their dreams and goals?

Don't let Excusitis take control of you. These are some of the common excuses we use. I've used a few of these myself:

- I'm too fat.

- I'm too skinny.

- I'm too old.

- I'm too young.

- I'm too short.

- I'm too tall.

- I'm too black.

- I'm too white.

- I'm not smart enough.

- I'm too smart.

- I don't have the money.

- I have too much money.

- I'm not good looking enough.

- I'm too good looking.

- I'm not qualified.

- I'm over-qualified.

The list goes on and on...

There has never been a better time to be alive than now. People are doing things that would have been impossible just 20 years ago. The speed of change is so fast that technologies that existed less than 10 years ago are obsolete today. Do you want an education? You can take courses from some of the best universities in the world, including Harvard and MIT, online for free. Do you want to start a business? All you need is a smartphone. You don't even need an office, staff, or a physical store anymore.

You're in a great situation!

But let me clarify something. I don't believe you can have anything you want in this world. But I do believe you have the freedom to decide to pursue it.

It's your choice.

By now, you might be thinking I'm ignoring reality but I'm not. I'm living out the reality I feel most conducive for creating a productive life. Abraham Lincoln is often credited with saying, "The best way to predict the future is to create it." That's my attitude. This attitude is much better than letting sensationalists, complainers, and worriers dictate my attitude and my future.

Talent Versus Skill

Since the birth of my first child eight years ago, I've been practicing photography with the same camera—a gift from my father-in-law. At first, my photos looked like images of ghosts because everyone looked so blurry. After worrying that our kids would grow up without any decent family photos, my wife gave me a gift certificate for a photography workshop. Fast forward eight years and I've gotten a lot better; I've even sold some of my photos in charity auctions.

When I posted pictures on my Facebook page, my friends and family enjoyed them. I received a lot of compliments. But the reality is I've been practicing photography for eight years with the same camera and same lens, and I still haven't mastered all there is to know about it. My friends and family weren't there when I took those photography courses, when I read my camera manual over and over, or when I was watching photography tutorials on YouTube. They also haven't seen the thousands of terrible shots I've taken. All they see are the nicest photos I post on Facebook. They don't see the work I've put in so they think it is just talent.

To avoid any confusion, let's go over the difference between skills and natural talents. Talent is a special natural ability or aptitude. We think of talent as something that comes naturally to some people who were fortunate enough to have been blessed from birth with a special ability. A skill, on the other hand, is the ability, knowledge, and practice of doing something well. While a talent might be natural, a skill is something we can intentionally improve.

My photography skills have nothing to do with natural born talent. My improvement is due to two things: an interest in it and consistent practice with the intention of getting better. A lot of times we throw the label "natural talent" over people like a blanket which answers all of our questions about how they made it to where they are. But when we do that, we're also telling ourselves we can't do it because we weren't born with some special talent.

Talent is a double-edged sword. Talent gives us clues about someone's success, but it's overrated as an explanation for success. I'm not saying being naturally gifted or talented is a myth, but the research in books like Grit: The Power of Passion and Perseverance, The Talent Code, and Outliers shows how much we disproportionately believe talent is the reason why some people succeed over others when there's a lot more to it.

The research done by psychologists studying elite performers shows that the way people improve is by "deliberate practice," which is a term credited to the foremost expert in this area, K. Anders Ericsson, who has spent over thirty years studying peak performance, talent, and achievement in the world's best across all types of fields. Ericsson wrote, "You need a particular kind of practice—*deliberate practice*—to develop expertise. When most people practice, they focus on the things they already know how to do. Deliberate practice is different. It entails considerable, specific, and sustained efforts to do something you *can't* do well—or even at all. Research across domains shows that it is only by working at what you can't do that you turn into the expert you want to become."[14]

I share this because it offers all of us an opportunity to get better at something, but we have to work for it. Most of us have been typing on a keyboard for most of our lives, but after a certain point we don't get faster—we've stayed at the same level. The only way to overcome that barrier is through deliberate practice and not just repetition.

Regardless of your natural talents or gifts, you still need deliberate practice to excel in your area. People suffering from Excusitis display an attitude, which believes they can't do something because they weren't naturally talented in that area, but at the same time, they've never been consistent and intentional about improving. They just say, "I'm not good at that."

Simply said, we quit too easily.

Well, no one is a champion at something from birth. Instead, you find that the greatest people in their fields also have a reputation for putting in the most time and effort in improving their craft.

So, what does this have to do with attitude? It's your attitude about something that will determine how you approach it. If you want to be a writer, a painter, an actor, a web designer or whatever it is you want, start with being intentional about becoming better—if you're serious about it. That's where attitude comes in.

Instead of just admiring people who are great in their fields, study them and look at the effort and time they put into their crafts. Don't use a lack of talent as an excuse for not improving or trying to improve. Attitude can be your competitive advantage in life.

Mixed Martial Arts champion Connor McGregor summed up this philosophy when he said, "There's no talent here, this is hard work. This is an obsession. Talent does not exist; we are all equals as human beings. You could be anyone if you put in the time. You will reach the top, and that's that. I am not talented; I am obsessed."

Change Your Lens

In photography, you change your lens depending on the perspective you are trying to capture. If you're trying to photograph wild animals on a safari, you use a lens with a long focal length resembling a telescope. If you want to photograph tiny insects you use a lens which looks like a magnifying glass, also called a macro lens. Changing your lens to suit the situation is critical in photography, and your attitude plays the same role in life.

Like a lens, you can adjust your attitude depending on the situation. Just like a camera can only use one lens at a time, your brain can't be pessimistic and optimistic concurrently. You have to decide which lens you're going to see your experiences from. This means at any given point in your day, you are being pessimistic or optimistic about what you're going through. According to positive psychology expert Martin Seligman, "Life inflicts the same setbacks and tragedies on the optimist as on the pessimist, but the optimist weathers them better."[15]

This isn't about living with unicorns in your daily life. It's about choosing how you will respond when life punches you in the face. For a lot of people, choosing a lens can mean simply choosing to be positive rather than negative, but there are more lenses at your disposal. For example, you can choose a lens that looks for opportunities everywhere. All lenses require practice if you want to get better at using them.

When I finally made the decision of intentionally living with a positive attitude and outlook, things just felt better. I still had problems, but I remained confident I could get past them. My circumstances remained the same, but I saw them from a different perspective or lens. With my opportunity-seeking lens, I can now see an advantage in most obstacles. It's a choice you can make as well.

Practice a Winning Mindset

One of the greatest stories in sports is the one about Michael Jordan's high school try out. I'm sure you heard how his high school coach cut him from the basketball team. Well, I'm sorry to break the news, but that version is not the full story!

It's true his Air-ness didn't earn a spot on the varsity team, but most storytellers leave out that MJ actually earned a spot on the junior varsity team that day. And that's the most important part of this story!

MJ, who was only 5'10" at the time, was devastated. Although he'd get to play, it wasn't on the team he'd expected. What made it worse was his classmate, the much taller Leroy Smith, did make the varsity team. In teenage MJ's mind, Leroy beat him, so this was personal. I'm not sure what MJ dreamed about that night, but he woke up in full beast mode. He committed never to let anyone beat him again.

From MJ's failure, we can learn about the importance of hard work, perseverance, self-improvement, stretch goals, and much more, but they all converge in one area—attitude! Even though he was upset for not making the varsity team, MJ decided to use his failure as motivation. Guess who worked harder than anybody else on the JV team that year?

Michael Jordan.

Thanks to that experience and his short height at the time, he developed great ball handling skills, which helped him when he grew into his 6'6" frame. Like Victor Frankl, Jordan learned what matters most is not what happens to us, but how we choose to respond that makes the biggest difference.

It was his attitude, not his talent that pushed him to focus on continuously improving his game. His attitude encouraged him to try out for the varsity team instead of the JV team. His attitude taught him how to embrace failure and use it. When he made it to the NBA and became a huge star, he checked into hotels under the name Leroy Smith as a constant reminder of the boy who beat him in high school. Leroy was a constant reminder never to stop working or take anything for granted. We all have a Leroy Smith-type experience in our lives, but the trick is to figure out how to use it for good.

The one common thread about the things we've talked about and will continue to discuss is they're all under your control. This has nothing to do with Michael Jordan, sports, or athletic greatness. This is about YOU creating a winning attitude, regardless of your circumstances, that helps get small daily wins that will eventually snowball into a phenomenal life. You can't be a Leader by Choice with a Leader by Chance attitude, but the great news is you can control your attitude!

Reacting versus Responding to Life

Once, I was having an argument with my daughter, who was around 7 years old at the time, about her homework. She didn't want to do it. If you have kids, you know what I'm talking about. After some back-and-forth, she finally said, "Why do I have to do it?"

I could feel my blood start to boil and I almost flipped out! But I held my composure. I'm not always this calm with my kids, so don't get it twisted, but I was this time.

I thought about her comment for a few seconds before responding. And then I remembered three words I read once—"You get to."[16] I said to my daughter, "Honey, you don't have to do anything you don't want to do. You get to do it. Not everyone gets the opportunity to go to school or has the time to do their homework. These are things you get to do."

When you think about situations from his perspective, you can quickly shift your attitude. As adults, we need reminders of the You-Get-To attitude as often as possible to make it stick. Life's difficulties, struggles, and frustrations cloud our judgment and perspective at times. For you, it might be a loss of excitement about going to work Monday mornings, cleaning your house, exercising, working on a business idea, doing your taxes, etc. Whenever you don't feel like doing something you should do, put on your "You get to" lens.

When this mental shift happens, we start responding instead of reacting to life. Responding is what happens after you've had some time to reflect and act. This doesn't mean that when something bad happens you bury your feelings. It means you stop to think about the best response possible before responding.

The reason it's better to respond rather than react is because it puts you in control and not your emotions. Emotions can be misleading because you often haven't had enough time to assess the situation clearly or you've made incorrect assumptions.

- You can react to something your spouse said.
- You can react to something your boss did to you.
- You can react to unfair circumstances.
- You can react to someone cutting you off in traffic.
- You can react to discrimination.

Or you can choose to respond in a way that is truly beneficial. It's a choice.

I know it's easy to write about this, but putting it into practice is much harder. It's hard for me too—my kids are great, and I'm better about taking time to respond when I lose my patience, but I'm not perfect. It doesn't happen every time. But just because it's difficult doesn't mean it's impossible. Choosing to respond takes deliberate practice.

It doesn't happen automatically.

The point is to think first and act second, instead of acting first and thinking later. When we respond, we're giving ourselves enough time to see the situation from a better perspective, which helps us get into the best mindset to deal with the situation constructively. It's like a photographer preparing to take a photo. First, he observes the subject so he can find the right perspective, then he takes the shot.

It doesn't have to be a long, drawn-out process of thinking either. Sometimes, just stopping yourself from your first reaction is enough to prevent a bad reaction. The more you practice this, the faster and more comfortable you'll become. As Zig Ziglar says, "It is not the situation, but whether we react negatively or respond positively to the situation that is important."

TIP: When I was a kid, I remember being told that if someone catches fire, you should tell them to Stop-Drop-Roll to help put it out. Well, I have something similar for helping us remember to respond instead of reacting. It's called Stop-Breathe-Respond. Stop; take a deep breath, and then respond to the situation. You can think about the situation when you take a deep breath.

Choose Yourself

After completing my undergraduate studies, I wanted to go on to graduate school, mostly because I didn't know what I really wanted to do next. I liked the student life, and I wanted to keep learning, so I figured grad school was the best option. Maybe that was my way of avoiding the uncertainty of real life.

I applied to about five different mediocre graduate schools where I thought I had a better chance of getting accepted.

Guess what happened?

I was rejected left and right! I was denied by all of the schools I applied to even the ones I thought would be super easy to get into. I couldn't believe it!

After being rejected, I recommitted to apply to graduate school. I was determined to get into a great school, so I decided against all sound reasoning to reapply the following year. I took the year to work and save up, and then I reapplied. But this time, I did something really stupid. Instead of choosing easier schools to apply for, I only applied to the best schools in my field.

Guess what happened this time?

All the schools rejected me again. Well, all the schools except one—my dream school, Columbia University.

This reminds me of when I was encouraging a high school student to apply to Harvard and without even thinking she quickly said, "They'll never accept me." I told her, "It's not your job to reject yourself. You don't work for the admissions department."

Columbia University didn't choose me. I chose myself first by applying. I bet on myself. And I bet on my dreams of going to my dream school.

And you will have to bet on yourself too.

Choose yourself; bet on your dreams. Not only did I reapply after being rejected, but also I aimed for what I really wanted. I was accepted to my dream school because I made a decision not to settle for life's leftovers.

Decide Your Worth

I know someone who owns a small business and he's excellent at what he does. In fact, he's probably one of the best in the world at his craft. People come to him from all over for his help and guidance, but after years of working at it, he has had little to no success in a field where he has the potential to dominate. His inability to succeed has nothing to do with his skills, product, or marketing. He hasn't been able to establish himself as an authority in his field because he doesn't value himself. From the outside, it seems like he doesn't value his services, his work, or his business, so no one takes him seriously.

His self-worth is so low he doesn't recognize the incredible value he can bring to his industry or even the world. Low self-worth is a common problem unfortunately. I've had it myself and at times I still have to remind myself of the value I can bring. There are so many people out there affected by low self-esteem. Low self-worth or low self-esteem can affect your pursuit of better opportunities, better friendships, and better relationships because you've convinced yourself you don't deserve better.

Without understanding the value you bring to the world, you can't position yourself as valuable to anyone else. If you're waiting for someone else to put a value on you, it's never going to happen. Choose to value yourself instead of hoping and waiting for others to do it for you. You have to find value in yourself before anyone does it for you.

Convince you about you. Believe you deserve better. Tell yourself every day you deserve better and that you are valuable. You can't have a positive attitude and negative self-worth at the same time; those two things cannot co-exist in the same mind at the same time. If my friend started to see himself as talented, worthy, and valuable, I'm confident his business would improve because self-worth is attractive.

Things Happen for You, Not to You

There was a point in my life where I believed good things were not meant for me as if I had some type of curse blocking me from being happy or successful. For a short while, I believed I was meant to have a crappy life, be broke and unhappy forever!

I lived out this pessimistic attitude by choice. I listened to brainwashing negative music and used negative words all the time, which made things worse. I was angry, hopeless, and cynical. And because I thought that way, my actions reflected this perspective like a vicious cycle. Then I gradually started shifting my attitude—and you can do it too. I started listening to inspirational talks and reading motivational books.

Over the years, I've basically brainwashed myself into believing everything in life is happening for me and not to me. And as I look back, I'm even more confident this is the case. It's like what Steve Jobs said, "You can't connect the dots of life looking forward you can only do it by looking backward." While I don't want to repeat the challenges I've been through; I know they've been incredible growth opportunities that have helped me get to where I am now. Those experiences have taught me more about life than anything I learned in school.

Now, I'm convinced all of the adverse things I've been through have made me stronger, wiser, and prepared for something greater.

Isn't that a great feeling?

Can you imagine what it would feel like for you if you had the same attitude?

It's powerful. You can make this attitude shift too, which is what we're going to work on in the following exercises.

Exercises:

These exercises are designed to help you change your perspective. If you've been journaling, write these answers in your journal. If not, download the free workbook from my www.leaderbychoice.me/resources and write it there.

1. What are 10 things you are most grateful for? Reread this list each time you feel like a bag of garbage.

2. What have you learned about yourself from your most difficult experiences?

3. Are you controlling your attitude or is your attitude controlling you?

4. In what area of your life have you been using excuses?

5. If you were a company (You, Inc.) what three words do you
    want your brand to represent?

Chapter 4
CHOOSE TO LEAD

"Before you are a leader, success is all about growing yourself.
When you become a leader, success is all about growing others."

Jack Welch

While in high school, my favorite sport was basketball. I loved playing, but the truth is I spent most of my short athletic career riding bench! During my junior year, despite my bench warming, I went all-out in practice, hoping that I could earn a starting position. For whatever the reason, I didn't earn a starting spot. I sat on the far end of the bench just hoping the coach would point at me and say, "Get in the game now!"

On the rare occasion that coach would put me in, it was usually in the last few minutes of a game, the garbage minutes, when we were sure to win or sure to lose. Even though I felt I deserved to be a starter, I never quit practicing hard, and that's how I brought value to the team.

There are times in life when you don't really feel like you're in the game. There are times where you unintentionally don't recognize the impact you can make. And then there are times when you have intentionally chosen to live on life's bench, just hoping that someone points to you and says, "Get in the game."

That year, when I was riding the bench and going home in a dry jersey, we won more games than had ever been won in my high school's history. I didn't get much playing time, but the commitment I made to practice hard made a difference to the team's success.

Don't be fooled by your title, income, or position; you're in the game and your presence matters to someone or some greater goal. You might feel like you're on life's bench right now, but you're not a spectator. You're in the game of life whether you know it or not. You just have to decide to create value and make an impact wherever and however you can.

What we're talking about here is leading yourself in such a way that you do the things that MUST be done in your life. You have to see yourself as a leader before you can start acting like one.

I love the way management guru Peter Drucker explains it here, "Worried that you're not a born leader? That you lack charisma, the right talents, or some other secret ingredient? No need: leadership isn't about personality or talent. In fact, the best leaders exhibit wildly different personalities, attitudes, values, and strengths— they're extroverted or reclusive, easy going or parsimonious, numbers or vision oriented."[17]

In other words, it doesn't matter who you are or where you are in life; you have what it takes to lead.

Don't wait for your boss, your teacher, your coach, or anyone else to grant you permission to lead. Take permission!

But first decide to lead yourself.

Don't wait for your circumstances to change before you decide to change. Stop looking for someone to empower you or turn you into a knight in shining armor. You have what it takes right now to make things happen. All you have to do is decide what kind of human being you want to BE. That's the reason we're called human "beings" and not human "doings." Decide who you want to be and be it.

What I Didn't Learn in Leadership Class

As a kid, I was a terrible student, so getting A's just wasn't my thing. It's probably because I avoided homework at all costs and I was lazy back then. That's another reason why the nun probably kicked me out of school. Since my grandparents couldn't read in English, I remember making fake report cards that showed better grades. I didn't share with them the real reports or letters from school; I would just pretend to read it to them.

That's awful!

But by the time I got to graduate school, I loved learning. I was still a little lazy, but not as much as when I was younger. I tried looking for easy classes whenever possible, but they were hard to find. But I did manage to delay the harder courses like statistics and economics till I felt better prepared. In the search for easy classes, I found a class on this thing called leadership. A retired CEO taught the class as a hobby.

We spent the semester reading stories of great CEOs who ran large multinational corporations, were well known in their industries and had enormous responsibilities. The people we studied were known all over the world and were at the top of their game. Some of them had influential and larger-than-life personalities and, of course, excellent leadership skills. While I really enjoyed the class, I didn't get much out of it. I didn't feel any connection to the leaders we studied. How could I, as a student, relate to CEOs running billion-dollar companies?

I now understand why I didn't connect with the central message of this class. I felt like a mere mortal in a land of Greek gods. By the time we finished the semester, I had a deeper appreciation for the study of leadership, but I didn't feel any closer to being a leader. While I did learn that leadership could be learned, but at no point did I feel more capable of leading. Years later, I finally understand why. The professor taught us academically about leadership, but he didn't bring out the leaders in us.

He didn't show us that we were already making leadership decisions.

Twelve years later, I'm a leadership lecturer myself so I have a different approach to my lectures. During the first class, I ask my adult students how many of them are leaders or are in leadership positions. Few, if any, raise their hands. This is because the mistake many people make is thinking leadership is based on how many people one supervises, the title they hold, or their status in an organization. Don't be fooled by this garbage.

Now I explain to my students that they are all leaders, regardless of their title or position because they have to lead themselves. Before you can even think about leading others, you have to learn to lead yourself first.

You're the leader you've been waiting for.

Leadership starts with a decision to lead yourself. Right now, you could be watching reality TV, but instead, you've decided to invest yourself by learning about leadership. I'm pretty sure no one is holding a gun to your head forcing you to do this. You're probably reading because you want a better life, you want to grow, and you want to make your life count.

Whether you're employed, unemployed, a teacher, a CEO, a janitor, a preacher, a housewife, you're a leader. You don't need to be a military general or have a busload of employees. Forget about titles, office size, and salary—those things are all distractions from the heart of the matter. Regardless of who you are or where you are, you are responsible for leading yourself into making the best possible decisions on a daily basis.

When I decided to act like a leader, I started feeling like one, which led me to behave differently and make different decisions. Did you catch that? I started acting like a leader before anything changed in my life. I didn't allow myself to be guided by how I felt; instead, I controlled how I felt by taking action first. The way you think affects how you feel, and the way you feel influences how you act and the decisions you make. When I started seeing myself as a leader, people started treating me like one. Don't expect people to treat you like a leader until you start acting like one.

Whatever hole, struggle, or circumstance you are in now, it will take self-leadership to climb out. But what is self-leadership?

- It means you're making decisions based on character and principles, not temporary feelings.
- It means you're focused on what's right and not who's right.
- It means you take responsibility for everything within your control.
- It means you lead by serving and not by controlling.
- It means you act like the change you want to see.

Is it easy?

Of course not. But like all skills, leadership can by developed with time, experience, and deliberate practice. But first, you have to decide to lead. So are you in a leadership position?

If you answered, "No," go back and reread this section.

Why Should You Lead?

The greatest movie EVER, Braveheart, is based on the life of William Wallace (1270-1305) a Scottish national hero/warrior, who went on a rampage to free his country from the British Empire and take revenge for the killing of his father, his wife and countrymen. The Scottish king at the time, Robert the Bruce, was a puppet of the British and needed their support to stay in power. This meant his job was to stop his own countrymen from rebelling or going to war against the British or else he'd be removed from his position.

In a scene in the movie, the Scottish king had earlier double-crossed William Wallace by not bringing his men to help him fight against the British and now he's having second thoughts about his decision. Here's a conversation between Robert the Bruce and his father:

Robert the Bruce: Lands, titles, men, power. Nothing.

Robert's Father: Nothing?

Robert the Bruce: I have nothing. Men fight for me because if they do not, I throw them off my land and I starve their wives and children. Those men who bled the ground red at Falkirk, they fought for William Wallace, and he fights for something that I never had. And I took it from him when I betrayed him. I saw it in his face on the battlefield, and it's tearing me apart.

Father: All men betray. All lose heart.

Robert the Bruce: I don't want to lose heart. I want to believe as he does.

Although this is only a movie, it's representative of the internal leadership struggle we face between the part of ourselves that wants to fight for what's right and the part that is only interested in self-preservation. Robert the Bruce did not pick the right thing to fight for when he double-crossed William Wallace. He was only interested in preserving his authority and position, rather than looking out for his people.

Self-leadership is hard because if you want to do it right, it means there will be times that you'll have to choose between two hard choices and one of those options will make things harder for you.

So why do it?

Why should you intentionally make things harder on yourself when life is already hard?

We live in a modern culture that increasingly places a premium on convenience and instant self-gratification. Leadership, unfortunately, doesn't have any of these options on its $1 menu.

What I've noticed is that the impact of making the best, but most difficult decision is harder in the short-term, but better in the long-term. But this contrasts with choosing the easier option of not showing leadership, which is easier in the moment, but the negative results build up over time. The real leadership problem we're facing as a culture is our inability to have enough vision to see the benefits of making the best decisions while avoiding the mirage of convenience and instant self-gratification.

As a leader, sometimes we have to see our decisions as a fight for doing what's best and not what's most convenient. Motivational speaker, Les Brown says it better than me when he explains that,

"Life is a fight for territory and once you stop fighting for what you want, what you don't want will automatically take over." Some people give up fighting and resort to spending the rest of their days couch surfing, shopping, getting drunk, watching porn, or living like zombies. They've taken the easy way out. They've stopped fighting.

If you want to make an impact, have influence, and gain authority it comes from having character, integrity, and being other-focused instead of self-focused. That's why leadership is so hard and success requires intentionality.

Going to battle is not something you can do by chance. It's an intentional and strategic choice you make that is backed up by a daily commitment. There's a reason you were born with the ability to take responsibility and make decisions. Everything good you want to accomplish in your life, like:

- Having a great family and marriage
- Achieve professional success
- Living in excellent health
- Starting a business or a non-profit
- Having great relationships
- Making an impact

All of these things require intentional, focused, and consistent self-leadership. Does it make life harder? Yes. But it also improves the quality of your life.

The quality of your life is a direct result of the quality of your decisions.

The reason for leading is not so that you can tell people what to do, but so that you can tell yourself what to do and have the integrity to do it even when it goes against your desire for instant self-gratification and convenience.

No matter where in the world you live, be excited to know that there's a huge leadership shortage and you can fill this gap. There will always be a need for authentic leaders. And you are the leader that is missing from our homes, communities, cities, and countries.

Don't lose heart by fighting for the wrong side.

The Responsibility Ratio

Over the past few years, I've been working with my doctors on some health issues related to high cholesterol and high blood pressure. I've had elevated-to-high cholesterol since high school. The most frustrating thing about this is that from the outside, I'm 6 feet, 160 lbs., and look lean and fit. I exercise 4–5 times per week and eat healthy meals thanks to my wife's knowledge of nutrition and excellent cooking skills. Plus, I don't smoke or eat junk food, and my alcohol consumption is limited to a little wine a few times per year.

But despite my healthy lifestyle, I have high blood pressure, so I have to take medication. And in a few months, if my cholesterol is still high, I'll have to take cholesterol medication as well. When my doctor gave me this news I was absolutely devastated. At that moment, I wasn't interested in having a positive attitude. I'm just keeping it real.

The doctor explained there was little I could do or change in my already healthy lifestyle that would cause a major improvement in my health. During a recent medical consultation, my doctor explained that when it comes to things like cholesterol and blood pressure, our genetics control 80% of our overall health. This means that regardless of my diet and exercise routine, 80% of my genes are fixed. He explained that through diet and exercise, my efforts could only influence 20% of my health.

I was distraught with my medical diagnosis, but after a few days I had a realization. After my pity party had ended, I realized the best thing I could do was to put my energy on what I could control which is the 20%. It might seem like there isn't much I can do, but that's a negative perspective. In fact, by focusing on what I can control (my diet, prescription drugs, my sleep, and exercise), I could maintain and slightly improve my condition. By focusing on what I can control I found hope. But if I focused on the uncontrollable 80% I would get nowhere.

I see the same ratio in life.

You can easily become distracted or feel helpless from 80% of the garbage that life throws at you. But if you take responsibility for controlling the 20%—the things you can actually influence and control—you'll come out with a much healthier perspective.

I call this the Responsibility Ratio.

One of my favorite people on this planet, the motivational speaker, Eric Thomas, often says, "Where your focus goes, your energy flows." By focusing your time and energy on the things you can control, you can find hope and move forward. You can control your attitude, your effort, and where you focus. There's so much you can't control about life, but focusing your energy on those things will get you nowhere. It's as useful as complaining about the weather.

Chris Gardner, the true-life person whose life was depicted by Will Smith in the film "The Pursuit of Happyness," said that his mother would often tell him, "Son, the cavalry is not coming to save you." He was so fortunate to have been taught early in life that it was his responsibility to make things happen. If he wanted to get something done, he would have to do it himself.

A huge component of choosing to lead is taking personal responsibility for every single thing that's under your control—the

20%. Taking extreme responsibility is the ultimate cure for Excusitis because it pushes you to do everything you can with whatever you have, regardless of external circumstances or your feelings! The Responsibility Ratio requires taking personal responsibility for your life, your dreams, your attitude, your relationships, and basically everything about your life that falls within that 20% sphere of influence.

I can't control how many people buy this book, but I can do my best to ensure it's useful to those who read it. I can also do my best to write something so helpful that you're inspired to stop reading right now and leave a five-star rating on Amazon. (No, really, go do it now!)

Focus on what you can control.

The Hardest Place to Lead

I recently read this book called "How to Be Like Walt Disney" and from everything I learned about his incredible life, there's one thing that stands out. Walt Disney's legacy includes numerous businesses, contributions to charities, and an unending list of achievements and awards.

But from everything he achieved, the most important can be easily missed. The book includes numerous interviews from family and people who knew him well, including his children. When his children speak about him they don't talk about his accomplishments, his business success, or his trust fund, instead, they say he was always home for dinner and he never missed a school event.

Even though Walt Disney was busier than most people, his family was a priority for him and it was reflected in his actions and not just in words. One of the things I see in Disney's life is that leadership is also about legacy.

How will you be remembered by those you spent the most time with?

What impact do you want to make to those around you?

The hardest, but the most important place your leadership is needed is at home. When I started my diplomatic career, I went through an orientation process that lasted several weeks. During the training, which is like Diplomacy 101, we learned about all sorts of things that are supposed to help us in our careers, like negotiating, U.S. Foreign Policy, etiquette, formal writing, answering questions from the press, working in emergency scenarios and a lot more. But despite all the training, there's only one thing that stands out to me years later.

I'll never forget the day our main instructor said, "No amount of career success will compensate for failure at home." For some reason, those words have stuck with me over the past 11 years. Throughout this time, I've confirmed it's so easy to be a public success and a private failure.

Now as a husband and father, I realize the most important place for me to lead is at home. Being a public success will not compensate for being a private failure to my family. In the office, I could bark orders at my employees, and they'd get the job done— (for the record I'm not like that). At home, though, that definitely doesn't work. I wish I learned these things from my father, but I can't judge him because he was imitating what he learned from his father. But as for myself, I chose to stop that cycle and create a positive one because I am intentional about leaving a positive legacy.

For me, all the success in the world won't matter if my family life is miserable. Am I saying my personal life is perfect? No way! But I can say without hesitation that there is zero drama in my life. I have problems and will continue to have them, but I don't have drama. Leaders lead, and this includes doing right by those closest to you. It means putting your needs second to your family.

Since my family is my legacy, this is where my leadership is most needed. This means I can't ask my family to do things I'm unwilling to do myself. I have to set the example for things I want my family to represent. I have to keep my word. I have to be patient, understanding, and respectful. It also means that when I mess up, I apologize.

Being a leader doesn't mean you walk around giving orders; it means you set the example for how you want your family to live. Let your actions lead the way. It's really hard to do this because you're setting the bar really high, but in the end, it will be worth it.

After living and visiting so many countries, I'm convinced that the success or failure doesn't depend on natural resources, culture, or history but on leadership. And if it applies to countries, it also applies to our homes. John Maxwell's leadership philosophy is, "Everything rises and falls on leadership."[18] That "Everything" includes our home life as well. Set the standard in your home and, like me, you'll find that if you're consistent and honest, you'll influence your family for the better. You have an incredible opportunity to make an impact where it matters most—with those closest to you.

It's Not About You

In college, I had this one crazy business professor. He was mean, he didn't take crap from anyone, and if you fell asleep in class, you'd wake up to an eraser smacking you on your head. But he was also the best professor I've ever had. He recently sent me a message where he asked about my life and how things were going in my career. After giving him an update and just letting him know that all is well, he said, "I measure my success by that of my students. When my students are successful, I'm successful."

That's what leadership looks like in the flesh. He's a professor and a life-long educator. He's not someone society normally calls a "leader," but he's speaking in leadership language.

At the heart of his message is not only an example of everyday leadership from an ordinary person but an example of the purpose of leadership, which is other-focused and not self-focused. Jack Welch said, "Before you are a leader, leadership is all about growing yourself. When you become a leader, success is all about growing others."[19] When you apply self-leadership, you will also have a tremendous impact on the lives of those around you.

Sure, being DA BOSS seems more fun. You don't need a psychology degree to know that achievement feels good. Success feels great, but the goal of leadership is not to appear on the cover of Forbes (but I have a headshot ready in case you work for them). The not so secret of leadership is that all of this is not for you; it's for the people you come in contact with. Human beings were designed in such a masterful way that you can find more meaning and purpose when you make your life about others instead of just yourself.

If you take a deep look into what our hearts are aching for, you'll find one of the things we're looking for is significance. That's why rich people want to put their names on hotels, university libraries, and hospital wings. We want to matter. We're looking to leave a mark on this world, but most of us have not found a way of doing it. Frustrated because we can't figure it out, we invest our time and energy into self-success and self-gratification. Significance is why some people donate large sums to charity, and why Warrant Buffet, Bill Gates, and Mark Zuckerberg, to name a few, are giving away most of their money to humanitarian causes. They've realized that the purpose of their success is to help others and not just themselves. Fortunately, you don't need billions of dollars to make an impact.

In the book "Man in the Mirror," Patrick Morley says:

"We often spend our energies to satisfy ourselves, rather than to serve others. Significance is not possible unless what we do contributes to the welfare of others. If what I do is only for my own self-gratification and pleasure, then I will never derive a lasting sense of purpose and meaning from it. On the other hand, when I embark on a task that will survive the test of benefiting others, a sense that what I am doing is important grows within me. And, if I make helping others my practice, a state of significance results."

Leadership is a strange contradiction. If you're trying to get ahead or want to do something great with your life, it has to become about serving others. On the surface, this doesn't make any sense. It's the opposite of the message we see in our society. But if you change your lens, you'll find it makes perfect sense. The more I learn about leadership, the clearer it becomes that it's about being selfless and not selfish. John Maxwell says, "The measure of a leader is not the number of people who serve him, but the number of people he serves."[10]

I'm not writing this book for my health or to get on Oprah's book list (it would be nice though!). I'm writing it for YOU! Yes, you!

I'm called to serve.

But this contradicts general cultural values, which goes against what leadership is really about. Contrary to the examples we see, when your life becomes other-focused instead of self-focused, everything changes and you start to change. You start seeing things you didn't see in the past. This doesn't mean we ignore our desires and ourselves; instead, we find that by building others we're actually developing ourselves.

The more I learn about success, the more I find that the people who get the most out of life or who achieve true significance are the ones who have made their lives about others. The list of people like this is too long to write here, but I see it in people I admire like Zig Ziglar, who at one point was considered America's leading personal development and motivational speaker, and who had an incredible career and life. It's no wonder that Ziglar's philosophy was, "You can have everything you want in life if you will just help other people get what they want."

I see it in Booker T. Washington, the first African-American to receive an honorary degree from Harvard. He was an American educator, thought leader, author, orator, political leader, and hero of the civil rights movement. Washington said, "There are two ways of exerting one's strength: one is pushing down, the other is pulling up."[21] The true measure of one's greatness, power, and authority does not come from the use of authority, but from helping others see their own strength. It comes from serving others and using our gifts to make a positive difference in the lives of others.

Exercises

These exercises are designed to help you discover what really matters to you, what your definition of success is, and how you can start to take steps toward self-leadership.

1. Are you a leader or in a leadership position?

2. How can you make a positive impact in your home, school, community, or place of employment?

3. In what areas of your life have you not taken responsibility?

4. Which activities should you stop participating in because they are just draining your energy?

5. Who is depending on you to succeed at life?

Chapter 5
CHOOSE YOUR MISSION

"The two most important days in your life are the day you are born, and the day you find out why." Unknown

Imprisoned in a dungeon with no chance of escaping, and awaiting his trial, William Wallace in Braveheart was being pressured to either surrender to the British king and live as a prisoner or be tortured to death. Undeterred, William Wallace responds by saying one of the most memorable lines of the film, "Every man dies, not every man really lives."

Did Wallace really say that? I don't know, but it doesn't matter because it's something so many successful people have in common. They lived like William Wallace in the sense that they all found a personal mission—something to live and sometimes die for.

They had a mission.

One definition of "mission" I really love is, "an important goal or purpose that is accompanied by strong conviction; a calling or vocation." There are too many people walking around like zombies because they either don't know enough about their mission or aren't courageous enough to embrace it, so they focus on existing instead of really living. To survive, they pour all their time and energy into distracting themselves from the void originating from an empty and mission-less life.

In this day and age talking about missions sounds a little crazy; after all, most of us are not being sent on dangerous adventures around the world, we don't have to hunt down lions as a rite of passage, and there's nothing left to conquer. But we still have a need for our own missions, though. The desire to find and live a special and unique mission is hidden in our DNA. Maybe it's a fingerprint left from our creator.

Finding Meaning From Work

One rainy day, I was giving a colleague, who was in the military, a ride home after church. We were talking about life and work, so he was explaining that he was tired and bored of his career after only a few years. Then, he said, "I have no purpose at this time." Even though he was kind of joking when he said it, I could sense a quiet desperation in his voice. Most of our life is spent working, so it's perfectly normal to want to do something you not only enjoy, but also feel it contributes to something bigger. Many of us, including myself at one point, are secretly struggling with a deep desire to find meaning and purpose in our work, but we're unwilling to talk about it publicly.

The danger zone many people fall into is believing their mission or purpose in life is only about what they do between 9:00 AM to 5:00 PM. Instead of having the mindset that you derive purpose from your career, what about believing that you bring your purpose into your work?

What I'm learning is that our mission is not what we do; it's who we are. Remember we're human beings and not human doings. In his book, "48 Days to the Work You Love," Dan Miller expresses a similar idea when he says, "A job should not define who or what you are. You should be able to leave today and not change the overall purpose or direction of your life."

Living your mission is about intentionally living your core values and your definition of success, and you follow the standards you've chosen for yourself, regardless of what the world thinks. Living your mission means going against the masses and leading yourself to where you intentionally want to go and not where other people think you should go. The greatest cure for living with a zombie state of mind is to live like you're on a mission. And if you don't know your mission, I'm going to help you find or create one.

The reason finding your mission is so important is because it answers the why, what, and how of your existence. If you don't know or have a mission, starting today, your mission is to discover your mission. It's composed of understanding these questions:

1. Why am I here?
2. What should I do?
3. How should I live?

The Misunderstanding of Purpose

"I'm so sick of this. I can't do this anymore," I told my wife. With tears running down my face, I told my wife, "I feel like I'm wasting my life with this career." I was having a major pity party because I was so frustrated with my career. I was whining and complaining because I believed I was living a purposeless life. Up to this point, I had read tons of books about purpose, leadership, business, personal growth, and psychology, so I had spent the past several years obsessed with the idea of understanding my purpose, calling, and vocation. I was desperately trying to understand how my talents and personality would fit into this picture.

But I felt so far from it.

In response to my pity party, my wife, who has some type of natural-born wisdom for saying the right things at the right time, said, "You are not wasting your life. You're doing what you are supposed to be doing. You're providing for your family." As usual, she was right. I had the wrong perspective all this time, but her words were soothing, like cold water over red hot metal. They calmed my anxiety.

You see my idea of purpose was actually working against me because I believed so much of the hype out there.

Don't make the same mistake I was making. Let's get on the right track.

Years ago, when I started my quest to understand my purpose; I thought it had to be to start my own business. That's always been my dream since I was a child. As I got older, started paying student loans, got married, had kids, and got a mortgage, I felt like a silverback gorilla trapped in a glass cage in a zoo. I couldn't just quit my job and start a business from scratch like so many bloggers claim to have done. I had to be more strategic, so I read. A lot!

When I was younger, I took action on a few business ideas, but they didn't go anywhere. I started an Internet company in college with the goal of helping high school athletes post their sports statistics and biography online, making it easier for collegiate scouts to recruit them. I paid to form a legal corporation, but my partner and I didn't take it much further. I just didn't have the drive or dedication to make it happen—I didn't have a strong enough "why" to push me through the valley so I left it alone.

Now older and wiser, I realize I can't throw money into any idea that comes along. So before jumping in, I studied. The more I learned about entrepreneurship, business, and successful people, the more I realized the importance of really understanding one's purpose and fulfillment in life. That's how I started down this rabbit hole of knowing more about my talents, my personality, my calling, and myself.

Eventually, I found myself in what felt like a deeper anxiety—a self-created mental crisis—because I was so closely relating my career success with purpose. What made things worse for me is that due to my parents' early and unexpected deaths, I have a strange relationship with mortality, where I feel like I'm going to die young too. I tend to feel as though I need to act quickly before it's too late.

I felt so worried my time was going to expire without ever finding "my one thing." It was through reading, coaching, asking questions, and prayer that I realized there's a danger in thinking my life's purpose is just about career or business success or any one thing. Purpose is not about doing one thing.

What I realized from my wife's few words was that we have multiple purposes in life and not just one. You are more than what you do for a living. The biggest game-changer for me has been discovering that what I thought was a search for my vocation was actually a journey to discovering what it means to have multiple purposes.

Jeff Goins, the author of "The Art of Work," explains, "You are not just what you do. You were made for more than just one thing. Your life is a portfolio of activities, all of which make you who you are."[22] I'm a simple guy; I'm not an intellectual, so I don't want to over-complicate this idea. Seth Godin explains it more simply when he says, "Your purpose is just something that you really care about." If you're like me, you care about more than just one thing. This means we have the power to choose our purpose(s) by focusing on the things we deeply care about instead of waiting to discover our one purpose magically.

As a husband and father, being loving and supportive to my wife and kids is a priority. Now I believe I have a purpose as a husband and also as a father because no person on this planet can replace me in either of these roles. I bring my own unique personality, abilities, values, and experiences to these roles. Not only do I have a purpose as a father and husband, but I also believe that I bring purpose to my career instead of finding purpose through my career.

These are all things I care about. So, instead of focusing on just one purpose—professional life, how about figuring out all the things you deeply care about and assigning a purpose to those things? And then you can use that to develop an overarching mission to live by which guides you to success in those areas you find most important in life.

A mission is a unique assignment or overarching life philosophy that pushes you to disproportionately invest your time, energy, and creativity on activities that you deeply care about. This becomes your legacy over time and gives you personal significance. No one on this planet can take your mission because it's the product of your life's experiences, abilities, relationships, core values, and interests. So while we have multiple purposes in life, we have one over-arching mission—to be a specific type of person, rather than to do one thing.

Why Am I Here?

"Why am I here?" is the question people have been reflecting on for thousands of years. But what if we're starting with the wrong question? We can get so stuck on this question that we just give up searching for an answer. How about if we changed it from "Why am I here?" to "How can I serve others?" What I realized is that in answering why I am here, the more impactful, energizing, and motivating thing we can do is think about whom we can serve.

Am I getting too philosophical? Let me stop and share a quick story.

Inky Johnson grew up in an American inner city surrounded by drugs, violence, and poverty. He grew up under what most would consider difficult, unfair, and even hopeless circumstances. Looking for a way to support his mother, he decided he was going to play professional football, so from that moment he dedicated his time to training.

Being short and skinny wasn't enough to stop Inky from pursuing his goal of playing high school football. What he lacked in size, he made up for with determination and commitment. Through a philosophy he describes as "imposing his will on life," Inky had a stellar career in high school. But at 5'9" and 180 lbs., he wasn't heavily recruited by universities, but he did earn a collegiate football scholarship.

His determination and motivation came from knowing WHO were the people depending on him to succeed. His power came from wanting to honor, help, and provide for someone other than himself. Months away from being drafted into the NFL, Inky was injured and paralyzed on one side of his arm, requiring numerous surgeries and intensive rehab. He was unable to play sports again, but the most amazing part of Inky Johnson's story is that his perseverance and willpower never let up despite not being able to play professional football.

Today, Inky is, by all accounts, a successful husband, father, entrepreneur, and inspiration. He is also paving the way for other kids from his community to go to college themselves. While his career goal changed, he remained locked into the power of who was depending on him.

So instead of asking why, ask who?

What Should I Do With My Life?

During a tour of the NASA space center in 1962, President John F. Kennedy saw a janitor carrying a broom. For some reason, he stopped his tour, walked over to the man and said, "Hi, I'm Jack Kennedy. What are you doing?" "Well, Mr. President," the janitor responded, "I'm helping put a man on the moon."

Some people have jobs, some have careers, and some have a vocation. A vocation is something you feel called to, work that you must do or something that feels more like a personal mission regardless of title, salary, or prestige. Career dissatisfaction may happen when we settle for a job, rather than choosing a vocation.

A vocation is a strong inclination to a course of action or state of being. The Latin root comes from *vox* or voice. Putting all of this together, finding your vocation is really a journey of discovering your voice, which is your truest and most authentic self.

Like the janitor, it's safe to say most of us want to feel like we're contributing to something special, to something bigger than ourselves that benefits others. You want to do work that matters to you. So it can be frustrating and even depressing when you're desperately trying to find that thing you were born to do, but you don't have a clue.

By now, you might be thinking, how does this stuff apply to people who have a job they hate? Do they need to stay there, make the best of it, and suck it up? Should you stay in a job you hate?

First, I have to say that whether you're a janitor or a CEO, you can find yourself doing work that matters or doesn't matter to you since it's based on the meaning you bring to the job. As long as you're receiving a paycheck, I believe you have to find a way of staying engaged and providing value. I know it's hard, but it's doable, and in the long run, it will help you as you transit to the work you feel is your true vocation. But in the meantime, it's so important to know WHY you're going to work and WHO is depending on you.

It's not uncommon, whether just starting out or after several years in your career, to become disengaged with your job. Sometimes, you just need to make money to pay the bills, so you take whatever job you can find. Wherever you find yourself working now, if you treat that job as an opportunity and suck out as much knowledge and experience as possible, and give more than expected, you can turn a dead-end job into a growth opportunity. Your current job is a training ground for creating or discovering your future vocation. When you choose to make the most of where you are now, you are actually creating future opportunities instead of simply hoping for them.

Victor Frankl said, "Everyone has his own specific vocation or mission in life; everyone must carry out a concrete assignment that demands fulfillment. Therein he cannot be replaced, nor can his life be repeated. Thus, everyone's task is as unique as his specific opportunity to implement it."[23] In other words, what you do between 9 AM to 5 PM matters, especially when you consider that you spend most of your life at work.

Most of us choose our career in high school or early in college. Unfortunately, it's unlikely that most people have a clue what their vocation should be at that point, or even after finishing college. However, we can find small clues along the way if we pay attention. While there are a few lucky people who know their life's work from a young age, for the majority of us it takes time, self-awareness, the right attitude, and stepping outside of our comfort zone to figure it out.

The difficulty with finding your vocation is that at some point in life, people believe that work is a necessary evil. They resort to collecting a paycheck, paying bills and waiting for the weekend.

But, it doesn't have to be that way. It's possible to find or create fulfilling work that matters to you. There are probably thousands of books devoted to helping people find their calling or vocation, so I'm not going to pretend that I can address this in a few paragraphs, but I can share a few things that have worked for me with the hope of inspiring new ideas in you.

While I do believe being happy is great, we can run into problems when we think that our vocation should always feel like we're riding unicorns over rainbows. The problem with only focusing on happiness is that it makes us too soft. We can't put up with the occasional pain and difficulty of finding and living our vocation if we have the mindset that we're supposed to be happy all the time. So rather than focusing on constant happiness, I have found it healthier to focus on serving, legacy, and impact.

Finding your vocation requires that you choose an intentional mindset of long-term growth, the right perspective, and self-awareness because everywhere you work is an opportunity to learn more about yourself, who you are best equipped to serve, and what makes you come alive. I've seen, heard, and personally known enough people who are doing work that matters to them to know that it is possible. And guess what? You don't have to quit your job and start a business tomorrow to make this happen.

The most important thing at this moment is to believe that it's possible to find or create work that matters to you. And for some people it doesn't even require changing careers. The second most important thing is to use self-awareness to gain a better understanding of your skills, talents, interests and who you can best serve. And the third thing is to surround yourself with people who are doing it. But without some level of self-belief, I don't know how it can happen. This process takes time and requires patience.

I wasn't born with the message I'm sharing in this book. What I discovered is that my life is the message I'm sharing. And I get to share this message through this book and in my daily living. My life is the message and I can bring it with me regardless of where I'm employed.

But this all came about because I believe that I could do it and I stuck with it, but there were times I wanted to give up on this idea of finding my message and pursuing greater things. But now I intentionally surround myself with people who have similar aspirations.

I know I'm supposed to tell you how I "made it" and how I now ride a unicorn that poops Skittles as we gallop to my penthouse office. But I can't do that because it's not true. What I can say is that in writing this book, I'm living my vocation, which is to share ideas about leadership and inspiring others to do more than they thought is possible. This is something I deeply care about.

I know most of us have to pay the bills right now and are just getting by so I can respect that. The priority is to pay for your food, shelter, and health. But even if you're in that situation, know and believe that it is possible to find something that is a better fit for you—just be prepared to make sacrifices and be determined.

Can you imagine for a second how awesome it would be to do something for a living that you're awesome at, that makes you feel alive, and that has a positive impact on the world? How would this affect your life? If more people spent time identifying their vocation, the world would be completely different.

The reason more people haven't found their vocation is not that it doesn't exist, it's because few people are willing to put up with the uncomfortable journey, which includes failure, risk, and some embarrassment.

The risk is absolutely worth the reward.

Consider the life of the African-American hero Harriet Tubman. Her mission at one point was to free slaves in southern parts of the United States by helping them traverse dangerous terrain to the North where slavery was illegal. After escaping from slavery herself, Mrs. Tubman put her life at risk and returned to the South to free her husband.

Instead of going with her, he decided to remain in the South because he was considered a "free negro." He could not imagine a better life in the free North than what he had in the South. He didn't think this idea of freedom was worth risking his life for, so he settled for life in the South. Extremely disappointed, but not defeated, Tubman decided to help free a small group of slaves instead, and she safely brought them to the North. From that point, freeing slaves became her vocation—it was her mission.

During one of her many dangerous trips to the South, Tubman was leading a small group of runaway slaves when they came across a freezing river. No one knew how deep the icy cold water was, so they approached the water's edge. With a mix of both fear and determination, Tubman took one slow and cautious step into the water and said, "If being cold is the price of being free, then we'll have to be cold." Freedom isn't free, and pursuing your vocation will require doing things that make you uncomfortable, but the reward is so sweet.

Since most of us have not tasted its freedom, we're unwilling to put up with the discomfort, so we settle. During the dangerous treks through the cold and dark forests, when slaves were thinking about returning to the South, Tubman would often remind them that while they were on an arduous journey, freedom was so sweet that no slave had ever returned to the South. Don't just settle for a job when you can choose the freedom of a vocation.

Vocation Requires Courage

There's a scene in Braveheart where a young William Wallace is dreaming about his father who had recently been killed. His father's body is lying on a burial table in a dark room when all of a sudden, he turns his head toward William Wallace, who is now lying beside him on a table and says, "Your heart is free. Have the courage to follow it."

Courage is the strength to persevere and withstand danger and difficulty. It might sound strange, but finding and doing your vocation—your greatest work—will require courage because it requires you to try and fail many times over. It requires you to have the courage to keep going. It takes courage to give it your all despite not seeing any benefits, money, or a clear reward. It's a mission.

I wish people were born with instruction manuals showing us what to do. I remember praying in frustration once, asking God why he couldn't just tell me what I was born to do. I was frustrated and struggling to find my vocation, but through experience I learned that in the moments we feel most lost, we're actually closest to making a breakthrough. As one of the students in my leadership course once said, "Some breakdowns can lead to breakthroughs." And that's what it felt like for me.

Work doesn't have to be just a place we go to exchange time for money. The average person devotes around 96,000 hours of their life working. That's a huge investment of our most limited and precious resource—time. The good news is you don't have to live like a zombie Monday–Thursday and then be a party animal on Fridays.

Did you know researchers have found that most heart attacks happen on Mondays?[24] They haven't proven it's directly related to work, but it's highly possible. Instead of dreading work, how about if you start seeing it as an exchange of time for impact, instead of time for dollars?

If your basic life needs are met (food, water, shelter, etc.) and you have access to the Internet, you have an opportunity for finding and doing work that matters to you.

For most people who choose this journey, it will take longer than expected, but the time is going pass anyway, so why not invest a portion of those 96,000 hours into something that can bring out the best in you and help others? I was expecting to write, publish, and sell 5,000 copies of this book within 12 months of typing my first words! But my estimate was completely off and foolish! By the time I actually sell my first copy, I'll be over a year and a half behind schedule. Despite my delays and setbacks, I have loved the entire process because it feels so good knowing that I'm working towards something I care about—even when things aren't going as expected.

The journey to finding my vocation has felt like hiking up a steep mountain with the occasional mountain goat pooping on my head. There were times when I looked up and couldn't see the mountain peak, so I got distracted and suffered the occasional stumble or distraction. In fact, at the beginning and even at the end, I was hit with so much self-doubt and resistance I started to second-guess myself, but I focused on taking the next step.

Every day you don't work toward your vocation or that thing that matters to you is a wasted opportunity. Your vocational clock is ticking, and it's counting backward from 96,000. Every hour you don't invest in stuff that matters is time lost that you'll never get back.

Maybe the thing that matters to you is starting that small business you've always thought about on the side, or maybe it's leaving your career to work in education, or maybe it's starting a not-for-profit organization that helps polar bears. It doesn't matter what it is. It only has to matter to you for it to be important. If you've been looking, but haven't found it, then I'm here to encourage you to stick with it.

How Do You Find Your Vocation?

Okay, so you're convinced about the importance of choosing a vocation instead of a job, but how do we do it? The good news is you don't have to quit your job now and start selling plastic toys made in China on eBay for fast cash! Some of us have strong interests and desires from an early age that offer big clues about our vocation. Our past is a treasure box of clues about who we are, what inspires us, and what pains us.

There's a strong possibility you've done something related to your vocation already, but you just haven't connected the dots. I've met people who are excellent at something, but since they do it naturally, they don't recognize that thing as a talent or gift. Describing the search for a vocation, Jeff Goins said, "Sometimes, all we need to find our calling is to see what's always been there. The journey of discovering my own life's work was not a process of dreaming, but the remembering of looking backward, not forward."[25]

That's exactly what I've been experiencing on my journey.

My first job out of high school was coaching a boys' basketball team one summer. I didn't realize it until years later that I really enjoyed mentoring, coaching, and leading teams. I felt like I was having a positive impact on the lives of those players and I loved it. I'm doing the same thing now, just not with basketball teams. Now, I mentor, coach, and lead adults and organizations.

If you're looking for ideas on how to make $3,000 a day on eBay, you've come to the wrong place. This book isn't about how to make money; it's about how to make an impact doing what matters to you.

Next is a list of six things I wish I had known before I started on my journey to understanding my vocation. This list will help you get closer to understanding your vocation and then what to do when you find it.

1. Look for Stuff You Must Do

Jeff Goins said your calling is something that you "can't not do." I'm not going to tell you there's one sure way to find your vocation. But I don't want to complicate it. Imagine your calling was a magnet drawing you in, even if your focus was supposed to be elsewhere.

For me, I am drawn to encouraging, advising, mentoring people. This comes naturally to me. What work or tasks do you just love to do even if what you 'should be doing' is something quite different?

2. Look for Pain, Not Passion

Dan Miller says, "Passion is something you discover after you've started something."

'Find your passion' makes for a great blog post title, but it's not practical for everyone or anyone I've ever met in real life. If people knew their passion from the start, they would have started a long time ago.

Instead, the people I know have focused on addressing a pain or some problem they felt compelled to solve. After committing to do something about that problem the passion developed. The commitment came first. Action removes doubt, so the more action you take the more clarity you have. Personally, it has always pained me to see people with tons of potential waste it.

3. What Makes You Come Alive?

Which activities, subjects or issues get you the most excited? This is important because it's another clue that will help you.

It's critical that you learn what really motivates you and why. Which social issues or problems make you come alive with anger, passion, or love? What drives you crazy?

When I speak encouraging words or share inspirational speeches, I get this feeling unlike anything else. But even after discovering this it still took commitment, deliberate practice, and courage to step out and do it.

4. Use Mini Work Experiments

When you think you might like something, try it out. Experiments help uncover what you're really interested in without risking it all at once or quitting your job.

Your current job or career is a great opportunity to experiment with things that interest you, volunteer for different activities you are curious about, speak with new people, and look for problems to solve.

For a while, I experimented with photography, but eventually, I realized it wasn't for me. Was the time I invested a failure? No. I learned what I don't want, which helps give me clarity.

Are there activities at work or school you avoid like the plague? Every activity—both good and bad—that you experiment with is an opportunity to learn more about yourself and how you can help others, which is a major component of a vocation.

5. Start a Side Hustle

Instead of making the mythical 'jump' I keep hearing about, why not build a bridge to your vocation?

I was introduced to the "side hustle" idea by Farnoosh Brock [26] my first business coach and mentor. A side hustle is a micro business initiative you do outside of work hours. With no pressure to make immediate income from day one, you can experiment more seriously with different businesses, careers, or social causes that interest you. And if you have a family, you can keep feeding them, which is something my wife appreciates.

At this stage, the goal is to get a bigger taste of your vocation while continuing to learn, grow, and be a valuable employee. I know a 'side hustle' doesn't sound as sexy as "quit your job and start a business now," but this is how I'm doing it and many others too. And I've been able to apply what I learned in my side hustle to my career.

Find what works for you and don't let so-called experts, gurus, and marketers tell you what you "should" do. Make a plan that makes sense for you, your family, and your own goals.

Even if you don't "feel it," start behaving like your current job is a bridge to your future vocation. Become a person who has a good attitude, brings value, and is known as a problem-solver and not a problem identifier. Then, you'll start to see opportunities and learn things you hadn't appreciated before.

If you have an idea for a particular service or business, you can experiment on websites like Fiverr, Upwork, Craigslist, and so many others. You don't need a lot of time you just need to work on it consistently. I wrote this book using 30 to 45 minutes max every morning before going to work. The problem isn't lack of time, but lack of focus for most of us.

Okay, so we've covered a lot of material on finding and living your vocation. Start by looking for those things you "can't not do," or things that you naturally gravitate towards. Then, tap into your pain as a possible source of discovering things you really care about. Personal development guru, Jim Rohn said, "We generally change because of two reasons: inspiration or desperation."[27]

Then we talked about finding that thing that makes you come alive. It doesn't matter if others don't feel the same way about it as you do. What matters is what it brings out of you. This is your mission and no one else's. Then continue to follow that path by experimenting with the things you find more interesting and gradually turn it into a side hustle. Once you've decided what interests you the most, seek to master that thing. Treating it as a hobby will get you hobby results.

Now that we have talked about your future vocation, I want to share the third piece of your mission: how to live. I know it sounds strange, but stick with me. This section will be short. By now, you know I don't believe there's one thing responsible for your success—there's no secret but in the next few paragraphs I'll share one common mindset or life philosophy I've noticed in super-achievers.

How Should I live?

I attended a conference recently where the main speaker asked the audience to raise their hands if they did not have a healthy relationship with their father or if their father was not in their lives. It seemed like nearly all the hands went up. It's so crazy, but sometimes we're so focused on our own problems that we completely forget other people are going through similar struggles in life. We give so much attention to our own problems that we forget about the things that are working for us.

This situation reminds me of something I experienced when my family and I lived in Cuba. We had a house that had an enormous mango tree in the yard. The tree was enormous so some of the branches rested over our roof. Somehow, one of the mangos must have landed on my roof, because one day I noticed a tiny green plant growing there. It was a two-story house, so I had no intention of climbing the roof to pull its weeds. Besides, without soil and water, I was expecting it to die soon.

But a few weeks later, I noticed the plant was alive and growing. At this point, I was eager to go to my yard just to see if this plant was still growing despite not having any soil or water. I would just stare in amazement wondering how and why it continued to grow. I couldn't understand how it was still growing even though it was in a less than perfect environment. All it had was sunlight.

This plant was relentless; it wasn't supposed to grow in those imperfect conditions because that's not the right environment. It lacked the key things I thought it needed to thrive like water and soil.

For many of us, life is similar. Sometimes we believe the things we lack are preventing us from having the life we want, but that's a lie.

One of the most important philosophies we can have in life is knowing how to live. This isn't something we're taught in schools so the idea can be a bit strange when heard for the first time.

When I only focused on what I lacked in life, I thought the world was conspiring to keep me down so when something bad happened, it meant that things were not meant to be for me. I lived up to that perspective.

But now it's clear that no one has a perfect life. Regardless of their Instagram accounts, everyone faces their own battles, personal setbacks, losses, and disappointments in life—some people just do a better job of covering it with cool filters.

And then we have some people who seem to have been handed everything from birth, but they still can't manage to make something from it. They aren't able to leverage those advantages into something better, so they become depressed and just settle in life.

The "how to live" philosophy has nothing to do with your circumstances, advantages or perceived disadvantages.

Like the mango seed on my roof, you have a responsibility to grow wherever life has dropped you and with whatever resources you've been given no matter how much or how little. Use what you've got. You grow only when you take advantage of everything you control and that's been placed in your life. Only then can you use those things for something positive.

But don't waste time throwing pity parties about what's missing in your life, who wronged you, and your problems. Use your limitations and don't let them use you. Develop an attitude that keeps you growing wherever you are right now, despite your circumstances.

Who said you were so special life would only provide you with rainbows? Rainbows only come after the rain. Who said life would be easy for you? You can accelerate your growth by putting all your energy into using what you've been blessed with, instead focusing on what you lack. You can choose to apply this growth philosophy to your current job, relationships, environment, and nearly all areas of your life.

Maybe you didn't get the love and support you needed from a parent. Or maybe you didn't reach the educational level you really wanted.

Perhaps you're struggling financially right now and can't make the moves you want.

Regardless of your situation, choose the growth mentality. You are not a victim of life. You are being prepared for something greater, but you have to choose to grow wherever you landed. Life is happening for you and not to you.

Choose to live with hope by focusing on the time, gifts, and resources you do have.

At the end of the chapter, I have some questions to help you in this area. The reason this is so important is that it will help you find or create your unique mission. And as you know, the antidote to living like a zombie is to live like you're on a mission.

Fight Like Your Life Depends on It

Let's wrap up this chapter with a word of caution. There's a scene at the beginning of Braveheart where a group of the village leaders have gathered in a barn to hold peaceful negotiations with British representatives. However, during the gathering, the British ambush the Scots, lock them in a barn and burn them alive. The few who survived are divided, scared, and unsure of what to do next.

While the majority of the remaining men are leaning towards surrendering to the British, William Wallace's (Braveheart) father says, "We don't have to beat them. We just have to fight." Your job is to fight for what we want because it's not going to be given to us. I know you're not a prisoner of an empire, but you still have to fight for what you want.

The act of fighting gives you life, and it's those people who choose to fight for something beneficial who make a positive impact. This must have been what Martin Luther King Jr. had in mind when he said, "I submit to you that if a man hasn't discovered something he will die for, he isn't fit to live."[28] See your existence as a daily battle to live toward your mission because that's the relentless attitude it will take. The goal is to fight.

Fighting is hard, tiring, and risky, but your life is worth it. The more opposition you encounter, the bigger your impact will be when you overcome. There's a mission only you can take, but you have to make a commitment to fight for it even when you don't know what it is. It won't be easy, but the difficulty in overcoming is a sign you're in the right place. It's like Jeff Goins says, "You can't find your passion if you don't push through the pain."[29] Use the pain as motivation that keeps pushing you forward instead of stopping you in your tracks. Don't take the easy way out and fight like hell.

Exercises

The following exercises are designed to get you thinking about your life's mission.

1. Let's imagine you're watching your own funeral. You see your body in an open casket. What words do you want people to use when they eulogize you? What do you want to be remembered for?

2. List the 3–5 people you admire the most in this world (or secretly envy). Why do you admire them?

3. Which projects or activities have you enjoyed doing or volunteering for the most and why?

4. What skills, talents, or abilities have others recognized in you or has someone asked you for help with?

5. List three things you'd consider mastering over the next five years. Circle the one that is the most exciting or the scariest.

BONUS QUESTION: Aristotle said, "Where your talents and the needs of the world cross, there lies your vocation." List three needs or problems in this world that drive you crazy. Why do they drive you crazy and what can you do about it?

Chapter 6
CHOOSE TO GROW

"God's gift to me is my potential. My gift back to God is what I do with that potential." John Maxwell

The Recipe for Success

For years now, I've been obsessed with understanding why some people have massive success and others barely survive even when they come from the same environment. After reading countless books on psychology, success, habits, faith, and biographies of accomplished people, I've learned many tips, tricks, and "secrets to success." Depending on whom you ask, they will probably say that success is about one of these things:

1. Hard work
2. Faith
3. Focus
4. Networking

5. People skills
6. Self-awareness
7. Focusing on your strengths
8. Ignoring your weaknesses
9. Self-confidence
10. Leadership
11. Honesty
12. Communication

After years of personal research, I found the big secret. Are you ready? The big secret is there is no secret to success. I haven't found the secret elixir that guarantees life will be a breeze and everything you touch turns to gold. Instead, I've learned success is more like my wife's delicious blueberry pie (my favorite, by the way); it takes a combination of specific ingredients like flour, blueberries, salt, sugar, butter, and cornstarch.

Like pie, success is made up of several ingredients mixed in at the right the time and in the right proportions. Eating one of these ingredients on its own is not tasty, but when combined, it's magical.

What type of life are you trying to create? Success and achievement are personal. There is no right answer on what success means until you define it for yourself. There are so many problems in this world because so many people are trying to follow in the footsteps of someone else's journey to success without actually thinking if that's what they want.

Personally, I define success as a life where my time is increasingly devoted to making an impact in this world by focusing my time, resources, and energy on people, projects, and causes that matter to me. I used to be in awe of "smart" people with lots of degrees until I realized intelligence doesn't mean success or personal fulfillment. Successful people, in my view, are people who are intentionally pursuing and living a purpose-based life.

With all that said, there is one common thread I have found in people who achieve above average impact and legacy. These people are intentional about personal growth. They're grateful for what they've achieved and learned, but they're unsatisfied with remaining where they are. This attitude can only happen when we choose to grow intentionally by actively learning from everything life has to offer.

As long as you keep learning from life, developing yourself, and growing intellectually, you're still showing signs of life. Personal growth is simply working towards becoming a better version of yourself so you can make the most of what you've been given and so you can have a greater impact wherever you are.

Update Your Software

I recently downloaded Apple's latest operating system for my MacBook Air, and so far it seems like a major improvement over the last version. These new features are so different, useful, and fun that it almost feels like I have a new laptop even though I've had it for over five years, which is an eternity in Apple years. With each update, the operating system gets slightly better because they fix bugs and add new features.

Can you imagine if human beings could "update" themselves like software? Think YOU 2.0 if this were possible just think of all the crazy things we could do. Based on the direction this world is headed with Artificial Intelligence that day might come, but for now, there's something you can do, and it doesn't involve downloading any software. One of the most powerful things I've experienced and that I've seen in others is a mindset that embraces personal growth.

I define personal growth as living with an intentional mindset that seeks to proactively learn as much as possible from life's experiences, rather than be a victim of them. I'm not a computer guy, but I'm sure that to improve an operating system developers look at the old bugs that affected it, listen to complaints, and work on minor tweaks that will make it better. Like a software update, personal growth puts us on a path of intentional and continuous improvement through learning about oneself instead of just reacting to life.

Consider what psychologist Carol Dweck wrote about the difference between a growth mindset and fixed mindset: in a fixed mindset, people believe their basic qualities, like their intelligence or talent are simply fixed traits. They spend their time documenting their intelligence or talent instead of developing them. They also believe that talent alone creates success—without effort."

Alternatively, Dweck explains, "In a growth mindset, people believe that their most basic abilities can be developed through dedication and hard work—brains and talent are just the starting point. This view creates a love of learning and resilience that is essential for great accomplishment."[30]

What I love about personal growth is that the ability to continuously improve is not only possible, but it's a choice given to you and me. Where you are today does not determine where you end up tomorrow. By choosing to grow professionally, intellectually, emotionally, and even spiritually you have control over your direction.

Your Environment Matters

When I lived in Rwanda, I had the opportunity to go on a mountain trek in the Virunga National Forest with the hopes of seeing mountain gorillas in their natural habitat. This forest is high up in the mountains where there is a never-ending cold fog and thick trees with branches draping like green blankets over the side of the mountain. There's also a lot of poison ivy there, which I learned the hard way.

Before starting the trek, the guide gave us some basic instructions:

1) Don't leave food or garbage along the trail.
2) Don't touch the baby gorillas, even if they come near you.
3) And don't make eye contact with the silverback. Look down at the ground and don't make any sudden movements.

Our guide explained that making eye contact with a silverback, the alpha male, is a signal you want to challenge him for his territory. There can only be one silverback per family, and the loser of these battles must leave, so they are literally fighting for their families and territory. About three hours into the hike, my wife and I were exhausted, and we wanted to give up. My jeans and light windbreaker were no match for the poison ivy attacking me from all sides as if I was an all-you-can-eat buffet.

After what felt like an entire day of hiking through this thick, damp, and poison ivy-infested forest, our guide quietly signaled us with a slow waving hand gesture to stop moving. Then everyone got quiet. In unison, our group of about eight people, lowered our bodies, took a few quiet steps forward, and, at a distance of about 20 yards, we saw a family of gorillas.

I don't have the words to describe just how beautiful and amazing an experience it was to see these colossal beasts playing and hanging out just like a human family. The babies were on their mothers' backs. The toddlers were playing and fighting. And the females were in a group watching the kids. It looked like a human family picnic except with massive gorillas. But separated to the side, all by himself, was the silverback. What a beast!

Only when you see this animal in its natural habitat—without the protection of a glass wall at the zoo—can you really start to appreciate its size, power, agility, and teeth. This silverback is so strong he was knocking over bamboo-like trees with a flick of his wrist. As we got closer, the silverback stood on his back legs, which made him look about 6'6". Then, he started beating his chest with both fists making a sound that echoed throughout the lush mountain forest like a calypso drum.

This was clearly a message to show us he was in charge. The entire group immediately looked down and, for a brief moment, I thought we were going to die! But our guide communicated with the silverback in some gorilla sounds and supposedly explained that we were not challenging him. I'm not kidding! He really did this or at least that's what he told us he did. What I know for certain is that after that exchange of gorilla sounds the silverback kind of relaxed and sat back down, but he still kept a close eye on our movements.

After an experience like that, I've completely lost interest in zoos because you can't compare an animal in the zoo with one in the wild. The zoo gorilla doesn't even know how ferocious he is. In the zoo, all they do is sleep and wait for staff to throw bananas at them. It's almost as if zoo gorillas aren't really alive anymore. They have no reason to be fierce, nothing to defend, and nothing to fight for. It's the same species, but a completely different animal.

The same thing happens to us humans and our potential. The captive silverback is a bit soft after being pampered for so long. He's fed. He's taken care of. He doesn't have any responsibilities or bills to pay. He doesn't have to fight for territory or protect his family. He lives in a retirement home for apes. He doesn't even have to fight for a female because the zoo will give him one.

As a result of all of this comfort and ease, zoo gorillas don't get to experience struggle, discomfort, risk, or failure. They're completely safe. The zoo gorilla doesn't have to prove that he's a beast, so he'll never know how powerful and fierce he really is deep inside.

He's in the wrong environment.

The same thing can happen to you if you're not careful. If you're in the wrong environment, if you're not being challenged, and if you're not developing yourself, you will never come close to knowing how much of a beast you really are. I choose to believe I only have one life, so I have to make the most of it now and see how much impact I can make with it. But I can't do that if I settle where I currently am and if I become satisfied with what I've achieved so far. You can't get to the next level if you stay the same.

Why Are So Many People Losing?

No one wakes up and says, "I want to end up broke, unemployed, lonely, unfulfilled, and in poor health," but it still happens every day. Why is it that so many people end up in these situations even when they don't want to? It's impossible to give one specific answer since we all have different circumstances, but what I can say is that personal growth helps us focus on what we need to do to move our lives toward something better. Instead of drifting through life, hoping something or someone drops a basket of opportunities into your lap, see yourself as a creator of opportunities.

Would you hire an architect who doesn't use blueprints when constructing a home? You wouldn't waste one second of your time because it's not worth the risk. It's the same for life. It's really risky going at it without some plan or idea of where you want to go. Isn't your life worth more than a home? If you go through life without any clear aspirations, vision, or even without an idea of what you want to accomplish and who you were created to be, then how can you complain when you don't find the end of the rainbow? You can't get mad for hitting the wrong target if you weren't aiming at anything!

Have you ever asked yourself any of these questions?

1. What do I want out of life?
2. What type of marriage do I want?
3. What type of money do I want to earn?
4. What activities are holding me back from making positive improvements in my life?
5. Where can I make the greatest impact with the skills and resources I have?

Did you know 80% of all gym memberships in the U.S. go unused?[31] The first few weeks in January are notorious for people who make New Year's resolutions to get in shape, so they hit the gym hard in January and then two months later they gradually start going less often until they stop completely.

Many of us, including myself, have made resolutions for eating healthy, exercising more, writing a book, spending more time with family, or starting a business—but we don't achieve it.

The reason is that having good intentions is not enough. It takes personal growth and self-awareness to close the gap between your intentions and your achievements; it doesn't happen by accident.

If you are working to create a better life for yourself, you have the burden of the responsibility and also the freedom to design it. And control the amount of effort that you will put into achieving this. But (1) you have to know what you want, and (2) you have to make it happen without excuses. This is where personal development kicks in.

Three basic tools in my personal development tool bag that have helped me in my journey of personal growth were: identifying my life's priorities, establishing my core values, writing yearly goals; and then constantly reviewing all three to ensure everything is aligned. This is the foundation of a simple personal development plan. You can add as much as you want, but I found these three to be essential for me.

From my office, I have an incredible view of this beautiful mountain with a snow-covered peak. As magnificent and large as this mountain is, it's only visible on clear days because on foggy or cloudy days it's completely covered. But on those days with poor visibility, I'm still amazed because I know it's there.

Having a personal development plan is important because once you have it written down, you learn what your priorities, core values, and goals are, so even when life's fogginess or distractions block your vision you can still refocus on the stuff that matters most. You might get off focus for a bit—I do!—but you'll get back on track because you know you have a plan.

Life is really strange because most of us don't instinctively focus on the things that matter unless we're super intentional about it. But even the most focused among us get distracted. Regardless of how you spend your time and money, your actions reflect your true priorities, so without a plan, how can you be sure you're living the right priorities?

One example is the person who works 60–80-hour weeks, plus weekends, and then doesn't understand why his family life is in shambles or is in poor health. He lost focus of what matters. A personal development plan helps you lock in your priorities and helps you stay accountable to them. The goal is not balance—the objective is to remove distractions so you can apply as much effort as possible in those specific areas of life that matter most to you.

You only have one life, so why not do a little planning for it? Most people spend more time choosing a college major than thinking about the type of life they want to live.

Kaizen

I know without a doubt that people can change. Why am I so confident about this? Because I'm not the same person today that I was 10 years ago. And since you picked up a book titled Leader by Choice, I know you're changing too. But change doesn't have to be this huge thing.

Let me paint a picture for you.

What words come to mind when you think about Toyota cars? Good quality, dependable, affordable, etc. The top selling vehicle in the world is consistently the Toyota Corolla.[32] Toyotas have a reputation for being the type of car that doesn't break down or have any issues for at least 10 years, but how did Toyota earn this reputation? And why has it been the top selling car since 1997?

Every time employees in Toyota's production line spot something wrong in a car, they have the power to pull a cord that grinds the production line to a dead stop. Next, the employee must explain the problem observed. Then they ask themselves five times why it happened. By asking "why?" five times, they can get to the cause of the problem and then find a way to resolve the issue.

This is the system Toyota has in place to ensure each vehicle produced in its factories gets better with time. But you don't have to work for Toyota to take advantage of this business process of self-improvement.

Reminder: There's nothing wrong with you, but there's always room for improvement.

Toyota invented this process called Total Quality Management, which is founded on something the Japanese call "kaizen" or the philosophy of continuous improvement. In The Power of Habits: Why We Do What We Do in Life and Business, an incredible book on habits by Charles Duhigg he describes kaizen as the process of getting better through "1000 tiny fixes."

I've realized that life doesn't get easier, but we can choose to get stronger. You don't have to live like a victim. That's why it's critical you know yourself and your habits, and understand your mistakes and your opportunities for improvement.

When we mess up, we need to take a deep dive into a pool of self-awareness to study our mistakes and, most importantly, understand how our behavior contributed to it. Our actions, including our mistakes, might be a habit by now without us even knowing it. Aristotle said, "We are what we repeatedly do. Excellence, therefore, is not an act, but a habit."

The craziest thing in Duhigg's research is when he explains that 40% of the things we do are based on habits and not conscious thinking, but the brain doesn't know the difference between a good habit and a bad one. Our mind will do whatever comes easiest—which is sticking with what we've done in the past, whether it's optimal or not—to save energy. So we need to be intentional about creating habits that put us on a path to success.

What's most inspiriting and encouraging about Duhigg's research is, "The Golden Rule of Habit Change [is]: You can't extinguish a bad habit, you can only change it." Becoming aware of our poor habits is an incredible opportunity to replace them with better ones.

The problem is most of us have not experienced enough pain, inspiration, or awareness to figure out how to change the behavior we've repeatedly been doing. If you want to change, it starts with an intentional decision that only you can make. Don't get frustrated when you mess up or when something doesn't change. Instead, get M.A.D. (Make A Decision), journal it, and study yourself.

TIP: When you mess up, ask yourself "why?" five times to get to the heart of the matter. You'll come out with a much better understanding of yourself and find the cause. Once you know why you do something or what triggers a certain behavior, you'll be in a much better position to do something about it instead of just continuing like a lifeless robot.

The good news is that self-improvement is available to all of us. And one of the greatest tools is your brain's ability to choose to grow.

We live in a world where we have to fight distractions just to find time to think, focus, and plan. We live in the "information age," but it should be called the "distraction age," since there's never been an easier time in history to be sucked down rabbit holes of porn, cat videos, political tweets, and end-of-the-world news.

However, there has also never been a more important time to unplug and be intentional about creating time in your life to focus and think. The future belongs to the people who take the time to plan and grow intentionally.

Run Your Race

One of the things on my bucket list is to see the men's 100-meter Olympic race up close with my wife. I don't know if you've noticed, but sprinters are not competing against other runners. They're competing against the clock. They are working toward getting their best time. Except for Usain Bolt, sprinters don't have time to look at their competitors to the right or left of them, since they're looking straight ahead and focusing on crossing the finish line. It's the same thing with personal growth because it helps you concentrate on your personal best and on your definition of success.

It's never too late to invest in yourself. This isn't about being successful in the eyes of others; it's about personal success, growth, and moving forward.

When we look to the sides, we're more likely to get discouraged and eventually give up on our dreams and personal growth, because we see other people who are achieving things we're hoping to achieve. Whether you are ahead of your peers or years behind, always remember that you are running your own race. Focus on your time and not your competitor. You only lose when you compare yourself to the people around you.

Once you lose your vision, you lose hope. Once you lose hope, you give up on life. Life without hope is just existence. Stay focused on your race. That's why personal development is so important. It's not just about having career success, owning a pet tiger, or driving a Bentley; it's about helping you find the hope and motivation needed to live the life of significance you deserve.

My Personal Growth Toolbox

Below are three essential tools that can help skyrocket your personal growth:

1. Core Values:

Have you ever had an argument with someone over something that wasn't at all a big deal to you, but for the other person it seemed as if the world was about to end? Sometimes in those situations what's happening is that you've touched a nerve. That thing you're arguing about is not a part of your core values, but it is for that other person.

Core values are guiding principles that determine standards for one's behavior, which are based on personal aspirations for character, fulfillment, and mission. When you touch on someone's core value nerve, they are likely to react more intensely.

All sports have boundaries and rules, so to win you have to learn how to play within those boundaries. Core values are similar to those rules as they are boundaries you've set for your personal life.

Some people keep score in the game of life with money, sexual conquests, and career achievement, only to later find out that's not what they were really looking for. The best way to keep score in life is to understand and live by a set of core values, which is basically a list of the things you'll need to live up to your definition of success.

Not only do core values show you the way, but also when times get hard, and they will, they set the standard for the way we should respond. For example, Martin Luther King Jr. believed "The ultimate measure of a man is not where he stands in moments of comfort and convenience, but where he stands at times of challenge and controversy." Based on his life, we know that one of Dr. King's core values was defending the oppressed and voiceless. He lived up to the standards that he intentionally set for himself.

Core values are the rules that define which choices you make and how you measure your own version of success. John Maxwell describes it this way, "Core values are deeply held beliefs that authentically describe your soul."

Understanding your core values, and those of people close to you is crucial because it makes you aware of when you're not living your most authentic life. When you're not living authentically, it feels as if you're not aligned with the right things. Knowing your core values helps you understand if you're working in the right organization, spending time with the right people, and can clarify why you feel upset about or inspired by something.

Psychologist Nathaniel Branden says, in his book "The Psychology of Self-Esteem," that we are "not biologically programmed to make the right value choices automatically." Instead, he explains, "It is a man's values that direct his action. A man's values are the product of the thinking he has done or failed to do. They can further a man's life, or they can endanger it." What I take from this quote is that we have to be intentional about identifying those values we want our lives to represent, but it will not happen by chance, it happens by choice.

Patrick Morley warns, in The Man in The Mirror, that, "We should look at every idea and theory we discover flowing through our minds and see which life view it represents. Too often, we see events and circumstances as unrelated and isolated when, instead, we should try to visualize how they fit into the big picture of our life view." Later on, Morley says, "We can know much, but if we do not use our knowledge to elevate ourselves—our mind, our soul, our spirit—to the highest level of moral good we can attain, then we are poor stewards of that knowledge."

In other words, if you haven't intentionally created your own set of core values to live by, there's a chance society is doing it for you. Is that what you want?

2. Priorities

I heard someone say that by looking at your calendar and your checkbook they can know your life's priorities. It's like Gandhi said, "Actions express priorities." But what we have to figure out is if your actions are the product of intentional decision making or just acting without thinking.

Even if you've never sat down and written out your life's priorities, your actions are expressing priorities, but are those truly the things you want your life to focus on right now? Have you intentionally thought about your life's priorities? I never considered priorities until I started thinking about my father's legacy. That's where I made the connection between priorities and legacy.

Recently I was in Miami visiting my old neighborhood where I grew up when my brother introduced me to the owners of a dollar store. I had never met the owners before, but that day I learned that years ago my father had gifted them the money to start their own business, which is still operating today. My father was extremely generous with his friends, and they loved him for it. In fact, I remember he was, at one point, funding a softball league in Miami all by himself.

My father cared so much about his friends, and it seemed like they loved him back. People would come to him for help, money, or whatever they needed and he was always there for them. He loved being the go-to guy when they needed help. Meanwhile, I never had those father-son talks or spent much quality time with him. I know he loved me, but I wasn't a priority.

It's hard describing our relationship—the only words that come to mind are a mix of loving and dysfunctional. He was never physically or verbally abusive, and I know he wanted the best for his other children and me, but for some reason, he just couldn't commit.

I'm not judging my father, and I don't hate him. But one of the things I learned from his life was the importance of having intentionally chosen priorities. But from my perspective, these were his top priorities in order (1) women, (2) money, (3) friends, (4) family, and (5) faith. What type of life can you expect to have in the long-term when your top priority is sex?

I'm not saying we don't need money, love, and friends, but the priority we give these things over other areas of our lives matters because if they're out of whack then your entire life is headed in the wrong the direction. My father left this Earth without establishing a legacy where it mattered most because his priorities were out of order.

I'm sure my father had intentions of being a good dad, son, husband, and all-around decent person. I think most people start out with good intentions. But your life can't go in the right direction when your GPS is set to the wrong destination. You might have all the best intentions in the world, but your consistent actions will always reflect your top priorities. If you don't actively decide on your priorities, your environment might choose them for you.

Your priorities don't just affect you; they impact those around you as well. I'm not here to say what your priorities should be. You can decide for yourself, but DECIDE. Don't just leave it to chance, culture, or cable news. I'm here to help you think about them so you can put them in an order that makes sense to you.

But choosing the right priorities is not free; it's going to cost you. It's going to force you to cut off all the stuff in life that doesn't matter. I thank God I'm not the same man today that I was years ago. I don't care about the bling, television, sports, gossip, girls, or partying that used to consume me. I'm locked into different priorities now, so I don't make time for things that don't have impact or significance. These are my priorities in order of importance, but they're changing so don't copy me:

1. Faith
2. Health (mental and physical)
3. My wife
4. My kids
5. Extended family
6. Finances
7. Career
8. Friends/Community

I'm not sharing this so that you can copy it, but to give you an idea of how I'm living today. It might be different for you.

Later on, you'll have a chance to write down your own priority list and then rate yourself on how you're doing. It's not about beating yourself up when you get off track; it's about choosing to be self-aware so you can make any necessary adjustments.

3. Goals

Goal setting changed my life for the better because it's the process that you use to take your ideas, priorities, and dreams from concepts to accomplishments. These will be your 1000 tiny fixes.

I had always heard about goal setting, but I never took it seriously until about five years ago. I used to set New Year's resolutions until I realized that was a complete waste of time. Once I started planning and setting realistic goals for my life, I realized that setting big goals not only pushes me past my comfort zone, but it lets me know that I'm working towards something, which gives me an added benefit of daily motivation.

Most people want to take it easy all the time and not push themselves, but that's a recipe for disaster. The most relaxing thing you can do is push yourself to achieve something greater because it gives you hope, energy, motivation, and enjoyment. Unless you're intentional and locked on to accomplishing specific things, you won't get those things done, and you won't ever achieve them because if it requires work, it requires intentionality.

I believe life should wind up, not down, as we get older, so goal setting is like a yearly push and reminder to get better, push myself, and accomplish things I care about. Goals keep you fresh with excitement and give you new things to look forward to. It's the perfect vehicle to keep you moving forward in life instead of just waiting to die. You were made to achieve, accomplish, win, and have an impact, but to do those things you need to plan and to be locked in on specific goals.

Did you know that over 200 million Americans have thought about writing a book someday?[33] Well thinking and doing are two entirely different things. Only a tiny percentage of those will actually do it. Not because they can't or because they don't know enough or aren't smart enough. It's because they haven't been intentional about achieving it. They stopped at thinking; they never went the extra step of planning it out and then starting.

Simply put, they have great intentions, but take no action, so they've resorted to making wishes instead of accomplishing goals. Dreaming is not enough, ladies and gentlemen. Anyone can dream. It's not about how much money, intelligence, or time you have. It's about having a plan, breaking the goal down into chunks, and taking consistent action.

This book started as an idea, which was then put into a goal. It took me twice as long as planned, but I stayed locked in. I have a full-time career, three kids, a wife, and tons of responsibilities so that I could have easily quit.

Goal setting is not just for writing books though; it applies to everything in life. Goals help you grow and reach further than you thought possible. You only have one life, my friend, so shouldn't you try to achieve as much as possible? Why not strive for maximum impact and achievement now, while you're still healthy and full of life?

Experiment and choose a goal-setting system that works for you. It doesn't have to be too elaborate or complicated. Find one, use it, and then tweak it and try again until it's perfect for you. And you don't even have to wait for the mythical day of January 1st. Start today!

Let me make one thing clear about goal setting before wrapping up. You don't have to make goals for yourself.

What? That's right!

Your life will be just fine if you ignore this section. Instead, you GET to make goals.

Wouldn't it be awesome to wake up every morning feeling excited to conquer your day? Imagine being internally motivated because regardless of how crappy your day was it doesn't bother you for too long because you're working towards something you really care about.

Would you feel a little more optimistic because you know you've taken responsibility for your life?

Wouldn't it be refreshing to stop drifting in life and move towards a specific direction by choice instead of by chance?

So if you're satisfied with your life and it doesn't need anything else, you can skip goal setting, but for those of you who want to see some changes or achieve new goals, this is what it takes. Goal setting is the actual planning process for creating a better you and a more exciting life. It's for creating You 2.0.

We can't plan life's unexpected events, but we can choose to grow by knowing our core values, intentionally setting our priorities, and creating goals that keep us excited, motivated, and challenged. The stress that comes from being challenged and pushing for achievement is positive stress, but the stress that comes from leaving everything to chance and not taking responsibility is negative stress.

Exercises

These exercises are designed to help you determine the core values, priorities, and goals that will help you grow and achieve. I hope you're writing down your responses and not just thinking about them. Come on! You're almost finished.

Don't quit on me now!

1. What are the core values you want to live by? Some of the things on this list will change over the years so don't worry, just start and tweak it as time goes by. Google "core values list" to get an idea, but don't just copy them down. Write down the top 20 and then narrow it down to the most important 7.

2. What are your life's priorities? Google "Ziglar Wheel of Life" to see an example of key priorities. Limit this list to 8 things max.

3. Okay, so now using your list of life's priorities, write one big goal or ideal situation for each one of them. These will be your big scary long-term goals. Then when you write your yearly short-term goals (one year or less), they should be focused on helping you identify the most important activities you should focus on next that will bring you closer to reaching your big long-term goals.

Chapter 7
CHOOSE TO OVERCOME

"Fall seven times; stand up eight." Japanese Proverb

On January 28, 2017, Serena Williams, won her 23rd Grand Slam tournament, making her The Greatest of All Time (GOAT). The craziest thing about this victory is that she played her older sister for the championship! These ladies have been dominating the game of tennis for three decades. That doesn't happen by chance or just luck.

When they were just a little taller than their rackets, their father, Richard Williams, taught them how to play tennis. He didn't grow up playing tennis, so his training was a bit unorthodox. Richard Williams didn't just prepare them to win; he taught them how to lose. One of the most interesting stories I read about their training was how their father intentionally moved the entire family from a comfortable and safe neighborhood to Compton, California, a place known more for gang colors and not tennis attire.

When explaining his decision for moving his family, Mr. Williams said, "The ghetto will make you rough, it'll make you tough, it'll make you strong."[34] And as if moving his family to Compton wasn't hard enough, he bussed in kids to their tennis practices and paid them to yell racist heckles at them. Can you imagine putting your children, especially girls, through torture like that? Not me.

But as crazy and unconventional as his methods were, it was kind of genius because he fully prepared them to embrace the world that was waiting for them.

In turns out, he was actually helping his daughters develop this thing we refer to as grit. In one of my favorite books of all time, Grit: The Power of Passion and Perseverance, psychologist Angela Duckworth explains that, "Grit is passion and perseverance for very long-term goals. Grit is having stamina. Grit is sticking with your future, day-in, and day-out. Not just for the week, not just for the month, but also for years. And working really hard to make that future a reality. Grit is living life like it's a marathon, not a sprint."[35]

But how does this all relate to losing? Well, it reminds me of a Bible scripture, "He causes his sun to rise on the evil and the good, and sends rain on the righteous and the unrighteous."[36] In other words, I interpret this as meaning that regardless of your wealth, your ethnicity, and your abilities you will experience disappointment and adversity in your life. No one has immunity from the unexpected events life can throw at us.

Getting punched in the mouth by life isn't necessarily the problem. What matters is (1) if we decide to get up, (2) getting up, and (3) what we choose to learn from that experience. This is all about how to lose or what we do when we're down. Explaining this mindset for losing through the example of top chess players, Duckworth said, "But when they lose a chess game, they know that they have no one to blame but themselves. They had everything they needed to win, and they lost. If that happens to you once, you can usually find some excuse, or just never think about it again. When it's part of your life, when it happens to you every single weekend, you have to find a way to separate yourself from your mistakes or your losses. I try to teach my students that losing is something you do, not something you are."[37]

Richard Williams taught his daughters how to embrace difficulty and adversity. In this, they learned how to use difficult and unfair circumstances as an instinctual part of the growth process, rather than see their situations as "the end of the world." He taught them how to turn their perceived obstacles into their competitive advantage on and off the court. Of course, off the court—in life—is where it matters most. Instead of being victimized by their environment, the Williams sisters have learned to use it in their favor, and you can do this too.

Instead of sheltering and protecting his daughters, Richard Williams threw them into the arena, but at the same time encouraging his daughters and helping them develop the mental toughness needed to be overcomers. He taught them how to focus and stay locked into their goals despite life's distractions because he knew their mindset was crucial in this process of creating champions. In the end, by making things difficult for them, he was actually protecting them.

Like the Williams sisters, you have the power of not just surviving, but of using everything life throws at you for your own personal growth and advantage so you can overcome. You can overcome by using life's pain and setbacks as tools to help you gain your competitive advantage, which will inspire, motivate and push you into a life focused on impact and not just income. This can happen when you change your perspective and see your circumstances as things that are working for you and not to you.

Anyone can lose, fail, or get punched in the mouth, right? But it seems as if it's getting increasingly harder for people to get up after falling. I have a theory that as our standard of living improves (comfort), our ability to handle adversity decreases. Is it because we've been too sheltered and haven't been exposed to enough struggles like the generations before us? I don't have an answer— just a gut feeling.

There's a big difference between surviving and overcoming. The dictionary defines "overcome" as "to get the better of in a struggle or conflict; conquer; defeat." But surviving is just existing or being alive. Being alive is good, don't get me wrong, but it's not enough. We would be better served by replacing the survivor mindset with that of an overcomer. It's not just about surviving failures and tough experiences and moving on to whatever's next.

Surviving is not enough.

Overcoming, on the other hand, means you get the better of a struggle and use it to your advantage. It doesn't mean that we will win all the time. Sometimes we win, and sometimes we learn, but losing is not an option. Like the Williams sisters, overcomers use everything life throws at them to learn and grow. Overcomers turn their obstacles and perceived disadvantages into their competitive advantages by keeping the right perspective, learning from their experiences, and finding something positive in every situation.

My Crazy Theory

No one wants to face adversity in life, but when it comes, you have the power to use it to your advantage. I'm not saying that you should look forward to adversity, tragedy, and a life of suffering, but when trouble inevitably comes, is it possible you can use it and not let it use you?

Yes. You. Can.

There was a long stretch in my life when I honestly thought nothing good could happen to me. I thought I was cursed. And because I thought I was cursed, I acted like a cursed man. But now, in hindsight, I have another theory that one day I'll spend more time proving. But for now, I'll just share it with you without having the studies to support it.

This is all based on my gut instinct, life experience, and reading about so many accomplished people.

You ready?

I'm convinced there's a direct correlation between your past pain and your future potential. In other words, the greater the struggles, unfair circumstances, or adversity that you've overcome, the greater your potential for doing remarkable things with your life.

Let me explain it with a comparison to something I read about weightlifting:

The author said, "By lifting weights, you are actually causing tiny tears (known as "micro-tears") in the muscle fibers, which the body then repairs and adapts the muscles to handle better the stimulus that caused the damage. This is the process by which muscles grow (scientifically termed hypertrophy)."[38]

Like the muscle growth that comes from tearing and then repairing and adapting fibers, you can do the same thing with life's experiences. Without the tear, there's no possibility of muscle growth, and in life, without struggle, pain, and setbacks, there's nothing to overcome. Those setbacks you've experienced are like steps in a ladder just waiting for you to climb them to the next level. It's about repairing (moving on, getting help) and adapting (learning from experiences) to become an overcomer—someone who uses everything that life throws at them as stepping stones for growth and strength.

To do this, it's critical you choose your attitude as we discussed. In this case, choose an attitude where you see yourself as a victor and not a victim of life's experiences. This doesn't mean we are fearless all the time, struggle-free, and riding on unicorns on the beach. Getting punched in the face sucks! I'm not going to say that the pain is not real or that it's just in your imagination.

But after your face heals, are you going to keep thinking about the punch or will you move on? It's a choice only YOU can make. As Angela Duckworth explains, "Our potential is one thing; what we do with it is quite another." She's confirming my point that YOU have the power to decide how to see your painful experiences, difficulties, and struggles. After taking a hit, staying down or getting up is a choice. Seeing yourself as a victor or a victim is a choice.

189

Process the pain. Go through all the emotions you need to feel. It's okay to have a pity-party, to fall down, and to feel pain, but you can't stay down forever. At some point, you have to stand up even when you don't feel like it.

Thomas Edison, a man known for failing thousands of times on his scientific quest to create the light bulb said, "Many of life's failures are people who did not realize how close they were to success when they gave up." It's in this process of failing and choosing to continue that something incredible starts to happen within us. I can see my theory play out in the lives of people like Gandhi, Martin Luther King Jr., Oprah, Steve Jobs, Walt Disney, Malcolm X, Winston Churchill, Abraham Lincoln, the Williams sisters, and so many more. All of these people fell seven times but got up one more time.

All of these people have been punched in the face by life, but they found a reason for getting up and were intentional about growing stronger from their experiences. It's a combination of perseverance, self-awareness, personal growth, and choosing to overcome.

It's one thing to get up after failing, but it's another to leverage that setback and use it to propel you forward. You can call it mental toughness, grit, determination, or resolve, but the key factor is making an intentional decision to grow from life's experiences instead of being trapped. What I realized is that when we have the mindset or the philosophy that come what may, I will continue moving forward, we are preparing for the future.

Purpose in Pain

When my wife and I lived in Japan, we were expecting our first daughter, but finding a hospital that offered anesthesia during labor was difficult. Generally speaking, Japanese doctors are reluctant to prescribe painkillers or any medication that numbs pain or discomfort. Pain medication is something given as a last resort in Japan. Eventually, though, we found a hospital that offered anesthesia for mothers in labor but only in limited doses. The hospital was much farther away than we wanted, but that was our only option.

My wife and I (mostly my wife) learned the hard way that Japanese doctors intentionally want mothers to experience some degree of pain during labor because they believe it's beneficial to the process. They think going through this type of uncomfortable experience gives the mother more understanding, awareness, and control of her body, which in the end is good for the baby.

During the medical checkups, my wife and I kept hearing this Japanese word "ganbarimasu." It means, "to carry through one's task, putting up with difficulties and striving to overcome all hardships."

Another translation is to "persevere and try your best." This word is ingrained in Japanese culture so you can hear it all the time in Japan.

The Japanese have so many different ways of using this word because they apply it to everything from pregnancy, to studying for a test, to athletic competitions, to recovering from a traumatic experience.

After giving birth to our beautiful and healthy first child in Japan, we learned that it's not that Japanese doctors just want mothers to be in pain, but they want them to use the pain in the process of giving birth to stay connected to their bodies, their babies, and intimately feel what's happening inside of them. Japanese doctors want mothers to give birth naturally when the time is right for the mother and the child and not when it's most convenient for the doctor's schedule. By feeling and embracing the pain, the doctors expect mothers to have a safer pregnancy.

I find ganbarimasu or this philosophy of pain management and overcoming so interesting because it doesn't just apply to women in labor. We can apply it to life in general.

It's so interesting to see how different the Japanese way of managing pain is when compared with how it's handled in the United States. For example, The Center for Disease Control (CDC) says on their website "Since 1999, the amount of prescription opioids sold in the U.S. has nearly quadrupled, yet there has not been an overall change in the amount of pain that Americans report."[39] Basically, people are taking more painkillers for the same amount of pain. There's a lot to blame for this that I won't get into here, but one thing this indicates is that generally speaking, Americans are becoming less tolerant to pain, or to be more precise, less willing to tolerate or face pain.

But what's more concerning is that when our pain is numbed, or we're drugged up, we can't identify what's causing the hurt in the first place, which means we're not in a position to deal with it effectively. Similar to physical pain, emotional hurt is an indication something is happening within us that needs our attention.

Pain is a symptom of something else occurring; it's not necessarily the cause of the problem. The situation gets worse when we try treating the symptoms of emotional pain with distractions like TV, porn, drugs, alcohol, over-working, over-exercising, and over anything rather than finding the cause of the pain. However, if we spend time identifying the cause of the pain, we can do something about it. There is purpose in your pain, but you have to embrace it to understand it.

Avoidance Versus Confrontation

According to an infamous poll, most people are more scared of public speaking than they are of dying. At first this didn't make any sense to me. But then I realized it's not the speaking that people fear, it's the anticipation of pain caused by the possibility of failing or being embarrassed publicly that scares us more than death. Pain, or the thought of it, can come from so many places like losing a loved one, unfair circumstances, divorce, lack of career fulfillment, loneliness, low self-esteem, embarrassment, etc. The common thread from all of these experiences is a sense of failure or helplessness.

Without having the self-awareness to identify the source of your pain, how can you treat it? Some people are in pain, but they don't know what's causing it because they're so focused on numbing it or avoiding the symptoms, so they never deal with it. Could it be because they intentionally don't want to confront the issue?

No matter what the problem is, we can use anything as a distraction from our pain. There's no problem with watching TV, using social media or working hard, but when we use these things to cover up our inner pain, we're avoiding instead of confronting. Without confronting, how can you find out what's going on inside of you? Explore pain; don't escape from it.

For most of my life I've hated confrontations, but there are some things in life we can only handle if we deal with them directly. One of my favorite authors, Kary Oberbrunner, said, "By choosing our pain, we can choose to step toward our potential and our ultimate healing—becoming fully alive. Think about it. The alternative to

194

being fully alive isn't that attractive. Numb to emotion. Numb to feeling. Numb to life."[40]

Sometimes we act as if we're so special that life will never punch us in the face. And then, when it does, the first thing we ask is, "Why me?" Well, why not you? What makes you think you're so special you can get through life without loss, suffering, or setbacks? Is it okay for it to happen to others, but not you? Do others deserve it more than you?

I'm not saying we need to become pain-loving freaks, but our time is better spent when we find ways of understanding and dealing with life's pain, frustrations, and struggles instead of numbing ourselves to it. The first step in all of this is choosing to be self-aware and embracing that pain. Only then can you start searching for purpose in it. And that's when you start overcoming.

Share Your Struggles

Once I was talking to a colleague from the military who was awarded a Purple Heart, which is the highest military award granted by the President to those wounded or killed while defending the country. [41] Without even asking how he earned it, he voluntarily shared with me his story. He described in gruesome detail how a bomb blast and scrap metal entered his body, the subsequent near-death surgeries he had overcome, and the extensive rehab he needed just so that he could learn how to walk again. As he was speaking, I was left speechless because I couldn't believe what he had overcome. I didn't know what to say.

Surprised at his willingness and the ease at which he shared what he went through, I asked him how was it possible he could speak so easily about his experiences. I had the impression most soldiers didn't want to talk about those types of experiences, so we should avoid bringing it up. But he explained that after losing several military friends to suicide after they suffered similar events, he realized that the soldiers who were most open and willing to share their stories were the ones who were best able to overcome.

I find this idea of sharing your story; especially what you've overcome powerful because it gives you more control of the narrative of your life. But this isn't just about people who survived near death experiences.

While completing my graduate degree at Columbia University, I felt incredibly out of place most of the time there, especially when I compared my life to that of my classmates who seemed so wealthy, smart, and well-connected. And after learning that some of my classmates could afford to pay for grad school in CASH, I was really in shock! Plus, as one of only a handful of black students in the graduate program at an Ivy League school, I spent my first year questioning if I really belonged there and if I had been accepted solely to help diversify the student body.

My self-esteem was pretty low at that time.

Gradually, I stopped wondering and caring so much about what others thought. But in my first year at Columbia I spent so much energy trying to fit in and being nice that it was impossible for me to be my authentic self. I had come down with a serious case of the imposter syndrome and I thought I could compensate for my being an imposter by being nice to people. As an author of a leadership book, I'm supposed to tell you how I've overcome this weakness and how I'm now suddenly super confident and got it all together all the time, but that's not true.

Even today, I still struggle a little with not letting others know too much about my personal story. I'm 10X more confident now, and much more self-aware today than while in graduate school, but like you, I'm a work in progress. At times the confidence has come from being forced to do things that push my comfort zone and also from those times when I deliberately pushed myself to do something despite some fear.

Have you ever felt like an imposter? If so, don't worry because it's normal and sharing what makes you vulnerable can help. Leading expert in vulnerability, courage, and shame, Brené Brown says, "Vulnerability is the birthplace of innovation, creativity, and change." It sounds counterintuitive to talk about becoming an overcomer, but at the same time express the stories that make us vulnerable, but when done authentically and with the right intentions you will see the impact, connection, and courage that come from it.

I'll never forget the day we were debating in a public policy class about welfare and what the government should or shouldn't do to help the poor. I was looking around at the students and listening to their lively conversation; but I doubted anyone in that room had any personal experience with the issues they were debating—poverty, welfare, and growing up in broken communities—but they were all prepared to provide solutions.

I couldn't stay quiet anymore. That's when I first spoke up by sharing my experiences growing up on welfare and the difficulties of trying to get out of the system. I explained that not everyone on welfare is lazy or just looking for ways to take from society without giving back. Some of us, including my family at the time, I explained, were actively trying to get out of welfare, but found it increasingly difficult because the system itself did more to hold us back than push us forward. To my surprise, several of the students came to me after class and expressed a lot of appreciation for what I shared.

We connected.

Looking back, that was a pivotal moment because that's when I understood the value of my unique experiences, background, and personality. There's power in sharing what makes you vulnerable. Sharing what you've been through when done at the right time and for the right reasons can open doors that boasting never can. I'm not saying to walk around telling everyone all the terrible stuff you've been through. But when done authentically, sharing your failures, vulnerabilities, and struggles can help you connect and earn trust.

There have been times when my life felt like a continuous cycle of struggle, but in hindsight, I now see how life has been happening for me and not to me. I'm not trying to be cute; I mean it.

I've been through:

- Divorced parents—before I could walk.
- Adoption by my grandparents.
- Losing two homes: one to a fire and one to foreclosure.
- Sleeping on the floor of a clothing factory for almost two years.
- Getting kicked out of a great high school because I was "too behind."
- Being arrested at 17.
- Losing my father unexpectedly.
- Losing my mother unexpectedly.

By the way, I'm not claiming that I've been through a lot. What I've been through is a walk in the park compared to what so many people are going through right now, but this is my story and my experience. These are the experiences that shaped me so it's important to know what events and things have impacted you too.

I don't want to repeat any one of these experiences, but in some way, and combined with my faith, each of these has made me a stronger and better person today. Despite what I have been through, I choose to see myself as an overcomer because I'm much stronger today and I have the self-confidence to know I can overcome anything that life throws at me.

The goal is to understand our emotions and not just try to be positive during times of pain, disappointment, and struggle. This is especially true for men since we've been taught that expressing feelings and emotions is only for women. That's emotionally unhealthy. As human beings, we have feelings and emotions that we should explore and experience.

The key is not to be controlled by our feelings and emotions. I need time to recover too from when I get hit with something, so I give myself a short window to complain, have a short pity party, or vent but then I intentionally change my lens (perspective). I choose to see life from the vantage point of a VICTOR and not a VICTIM. And you can do the same. Sharing my struggles, in person or writing, has definitely been helpful in helping me live like an overcomer. And you don't have to have a tragic or super inspirational story; it just needs to be authentic to your experience.

The Advantage of Disadvantage

Society passes out labels like candy and sometimes we accept them without thinking. Labels are supposed to help make things easier for us by categorizing things, people, and experience, but some labels can be dangerous when they limit your perspective or vision. I recently read that even in the world of psychology, experts have mixed views on labeling patients because of the permanent impact those descriptions can have, especially if the patient is misdiagnosed.

One of the things I hate about our political system is the pressure to label my views as either Democrat or Republican, even though I have ideas that go against both parties. The danger with labels is that they box in our freedom to think, process, and live.

Here is a short list of some common labels:

- Poor or economically disadvantaged
- Physically challenged
- Intellectually challenged
- Divorced

- Addict/Alcoholic
- Black/White/Hispanic/Asian
- Drop-out
- Elderly
- Millennial
- Immigrant

The problem is that these labels categorize people who are dynamic and not meant to be grouped into fictitious categories permanently. Some labels are needed to self-assess and then move on like "alcoholic." But most labels are like geographic borders in the sense that they keep people confined within a limited space.

Some labels categorize our experiences in such a way that they're supposed to alert others to someone who is seen as more vulnerable. But these labels also reinforce a victim mentality to the person who accepts the label. After a while, you start instinctively responding according to the limits of that label. If you accept any of these labels, it reinforces stereotypes and expectations created by a society that limits what you are and what you can achieve.

Labels allow others to define your story.

The obstacle or the problem is not the apparent disadvantage you might be experiencing. The actual problem is our inability to see through that label and flipping it from a disadvantage into your competitive advantage.

I'm convinced people who grew up under difficult circumstances or who have faced any type of adversity have been given an incredible opportunity to turn that pain into internal motivation.

The motivation I'm referring to comes from one's ability to turn those disadvantages into fuel for winning in life. Instead of running away or hiding, we can embrace our struggles and learn to use them for us, instead of against us. The attitude that is most helpful is one where we believe we can turn ALL of our setbacks and struggles into advantages. It's a philosophy for living.

If you've struggled, faced adversity, or dealt with unfair circumstances, you have an education that can't be bought or learned in a school. You graduated with a degree from the School of Hard Knocks! Congratulations. Use it. And if used properly, this degree can take you places a classroom education cannot.

You haven't come this far in life just to stop now.

When you're going through hard times, it might seem like the end of the world at that moment, but when you persevere you come out a different person because of what you've learned along the way, and if you use that knowledge to your advantage you can take things to another level. Surviving is not enough when overcoming is an option. If you are not learning from your experiences, you are missing out on a free education.

Turn Setbacks into Set Ups

Recently, my five-year-old daughter learned that her teacher passed away unexpectedly. Explaining the concept of death to a child was harder than I thought it would be. Some parents found it so difficult they waited for the school to tell their children. To help the teachers and students cope with this tragedy, the school brought in a grief counselor to speak with anyone who needed additional help.

When the counselor was meeting with a group of parents, one of the things she explained was the importance of being honest about death with children. She said that in the process of overcoming grief, it's crucial for children to hear two truths: (1) the person is dead and (2) this person is not coming back.

Telling this to anyone who's lost someone they care about is hard, but saying it to my five-year-old who doesn't really understand tragedy and death was difficult at best. The counselor explained that children need to hear this to continue with the grieving process and eventually overcome this emotional wound.

After she had finished taking questions and everyone left, I asked the counselor, how could my wife and I use the teacher's death as an opportunity to show my daughter how to really live and make the most of life? I asked this because I don't want my daughter just to heal and move on; I want to her to be an overcomer and not just a survivor. I want her to learn how to take whatever life throws at her and use it, instead of being a victim of it.

Excited by the question, the counselor explained that life is like a game and we have to do everything possible to make the most of this life because we don't know what's coming next. She said, "Kids know and love a game, so speak to them in the language of games. Once the game of life is over, you will not have a second chance to live it, so what can you do now to make the most of this life? What do you have to learn? What do you want to do with your time? What's the greatest vision you can create for your life?"

For you and I, it's the same thing. We don't have to wait for a tragedy to strike to appreciate life. Regardless of your faith, one thing unites us all. One day you will die and you will not come back. But dying is the easy part. How can we take this one life and make the most of it?

The Gift of Mortality

Once during my annual medical checkup, my doctor asked me those routine, but intrusive, health-related questions. You know…

Are you sexually active with multiple partners?

Do you exercise regularly?

Do you get enough sleep?

And then the question I hate the most—my parents' medical history. Even though I know it's coming, this question always seems to get me by surprise. I'm really good at deflecting conversations on topics I don't want to discuss during small talk—like anything about my parents. At this point, it comes naturally to me. But at the doctor's office, it's impossible—I have to explain my parent's story in detail that makes me really uncomfortable.

On this day, I said, "I don't know anything about my parents' medical history." I explained that my father appeared to be in excellent health, but he drowned in a boating accident in his 40s. He suffered a concussion when the boat he was riding flipped. He suffered a concussion after getting hit in the head with something and then he stopped swimming, so he drowned."

Then she asked, "What about your mother?"

I explained, "Well, my mother passed away young as well. She had a respiratory disease that she acquired after taking diet pills called fen-phen. Her symptoms started with a shortness of breath, loss of energy, and exhaustion weeks after taking the drug. Once having identified the medical problem, doctors said it was untreatable. Within a few years, she went from a healthy and lively woman to someone needing a wheelchair to get around, an oxygen tank to breathe, and medication delivered through a hole in her chest."

By this point, doctors normally respond with, "That's awful," or, "I'm so sorry to hear that." But this doctor was different.

She said, "Wow, you've had some bad luck!"

On the drive home when I thought about her comment I wanted to have responded with a "Go to hell!" and slam the door on the way out without paying the bill. But lucky for me, I need time to process the things people say so I don't instinctively react quickly with emotions. I have to reflect on things for a while, before I can respond.

But on the drive home, when my brain had time to process her comment, it bothered me down to my soul. That's the only way I can explain it. I'm not sure what bothered me so much about her comment. Maybe it was her casual attitude about my parents' death or maybe she actually believes I'm an unlucky person.

Whatever it is, she's wrong!

Yes, my parents' deaths were tragedies. Even though I always lived with my grandparents, my parents' deaths left me in a state of shock, sadness, and a near depression. At the time, I felt like my world was collapsing, so for a while, I did feel unlucky. I believe my faith in God helped me greatly during those experiences.

But now I also realize that their deaths were an awakening that gave me an urgency to live. I don't have to jump out of planes, bungee jump, or dive off cliffs to feel alive. All I have to do is embrace my mortality and shortness of life. The biggest problem in life is not death; it's living as if death is not coming.

If I had the chance to have that conversation again with that doctor, I would say something like:

"No doctor, I'm not unlucky at all. In fact, I'm one of the most fortunate people in the world because I've been able to develop an appreciation for life that most people never get to experience until it's too late.

There's a huge difference between living and existing, and in my parents' unexpected deaths I gained an appreciation for life and purpose that most people only develop when it's almost time for them to leave this world. So my question to you doctor is, are you living or just existing?"

Like William Wallace said, "Every man dies; not every man really lives." Becoming aware of your mortality is a gift because it helps us think about what living really means. Reflecting on your mortality is not supposed to depress you. On the contrary, let it encourage you.

This topic reminds me of something my sister posted on Facebook once. She wrote, "Life becomes more special when you realize that you will never live the same moment twice." In becoming aware of your mortality, you can become more intentional about your entire life, your family relationships, and even how you use your gifts of time, talents, and money. Zig Ziglar said, "I've done the math, and it's clear that we will spend more time dead than alive." We don't need a disaster to strike to appreciate life. We just have to reflect on our impending mortality and what we want to make of our limited time.

One of my favorite proverbs says, "Teach me, Lord, to number my days so that I may gain a heart of wisdom."[42] I think this means that when we reflect on just how short our life really is it can help us focus on the essential. And that's wisdom. Thinking about the end can help us live now.

You've Come Too Far

One of my favorite stories is of Louis Zamperini, which is depicted in the film Unbroken. Zamperini was a juvenile delinquent struggling to find himself. He was always getting into trouble with the police, running scams on anyone he could, and stealing.

Eventually, Zamperini joined the military and had one near death experience after another. He survived a plane crash, 45 days lost at sea (the longest in recorded military history), and a barrage of physical and psychological torture as a prisoner of war under the Japanese. After the military, he suffered from symptoms similar to those of Post-Traumatic Stress Disorder (PTSD) but this wasn't a diagnosis back then. Zamperini tried to numb his pain through the distraction of alcohol.

But one day, at the urging of his wife, Zamperini went to listen to pastor Billy Graham. After which, Louis had a breakthrough. He dedicated his life to the Christian faith and realized that everything he had survived was not just a mere coincidence; he was meant to survive so that he could use those experiences to help others. He felt he had survived so much in life because he had a higher purpose. That's when Zamperini decided to focus on helping troubled youth; he decided to use his pain to help others, he went from survivor to overcomer.

In this program, kids spend a week living in nature where they are tested and challenged —but the true battle occurs in their heads. The goal for them, at the end of the week, is to reflect on all that they accomplished and overcame in the wild. And by doing this, Zamperini can show them the same lesson he learned—that we can accomplish things we never thought possible, and through those experiences, we can gain confidence and learn how to do greater things.

So how does this story relate to you?

Like Zamperini, I'm sure you've survived your fair share of haters, adversity, and punches in the face. They probably weren't as dramatic as Zamperini's, but, regardless, it's your story and you were affected. You haven't survived so much and come this far to quit now. There's more to your story. There's purpose for your life, and when you decide to help others in some way, you take your story from that of a survivor to that of an overcomer. That's the moment you realize your life and everything you've overcome is not just about you.

Exercises

Use these exercises to help you see the things you've been through from a different perspective. If you want to get the most from these exercises you have to write your answers. Don't think; just write and let the pen do the thinking.

1. What excuses have you been using for not accomplishing the things you said you wanted to do?
2. Draw a timeline with the seven most challenging, yet important events in your life that you have overcome.
3. What advantages have you gained in life thanks to the hardships and challenges you've faced?
4. If your doctor says you have five years to live, how would you spend your remaining time?
5. If you could speak with your future self who is old and about to die, what advice would you give yourself for today?

Conclusion
TO BE OR NOT TO BE

Once I asked the number-two person in the organization where I was working if he had any professional advice for me. I was expecting something really deep, but all he said was, "Look the part."

I was so disappointed because I thought that was the shallowest thing I'd ever heard. It didn't make sense at the time. But I get it now. What I think he meant was that I have to look and act now for the position I want in the future. But the advice he gave me isn't just about work. It applies to living and leadership as well.

Simply said, we can start acting now like the type of person we'd like to become one day. This idea basically comes down to you making a daily decision to be the person you hope to become in the future now.

This idea was confirmed to me in a recent conversation with my wife. I was talking about work when I realized that one of the most important things I had done to increase my confidence and preparedness for professional growth is when I decided I would start behaving like a leader instead of waiting for someone to come and show me the way.

Earlier in my career, I wasn't surrounded by the type of leadership I was expecting. But it isn't anyone's fault. In fact, it was my fault for relying on expectations instead of doing something about it. So now instead of waiting for a great boss, supervisor, or colleagues I act like the person I am looking for.

I started acting the part before I had it.

Today, I'm currently leading a team of around 200 employees, I have more confidence, and I see myself as a difference maker. But I started acting like a leader at work before my title and responsibilities changed.

I started acting like a better husband before my wife made any changes.

I started acting like a better father before I felt ready or comfortable.

I started acting like an honest, hardworking, and committed person before I was.

I started teaching leadership before I was ready.

I started writing this book before I was ready.

I became the change I wanted to see in my place of employment, in my home, and in my community BEFORE I was ready.

When I started acting like the leader I wanted to become, I noticed that more people started treating me like one. My wife noticed it too so this isn't something just in my imagination.

I had to see myself as a leader and difference-maker first before others would see it in me. This is at the heart of what we've been talking about—personal transformation. Motivation can be external, but at some point, in order for the change to be permanent, it has to originate from within.

You don't have to wait for something to happen or some drastic event in your life before you decide to become a Leader by Choice. God, the universe, unicorns or whatever you believe has given you the freedom and authority to be something. You get to decide what type of person you will be so why not choose the best version there can be?

What Do You Want to Be?

Adults love asking children, "What do you want to be when you grow up?" But among adults, for some reason, we don't ask this question anymore. Why? Is it because adults should have figured it all out by some specific age and know everything there is to know about life, career, and family? It's a shame that we stopped asking these types of questions to adults since finishing school doesn't mean we finished our education.

Did the journey toward us "being" stop at some magical moment or when we hit the legal age? Did all adults, all of a sudden, figure out who they were meant to be? Of course not. But for some reason many of us stopped asking, growing, and expecting more from ourselves. We built a pretty glass box to live inside of.

Maybe it's because we're too embarrassed to admit we haven't figured it out. Or perhaps the subtle pressures of mortgages, responsibilities, and our culture's expectations just distracted us. Or maybe it's because no one ever said you can and should lead, regardless of your title, position, or status.

In What to Say When You Talk to Yourself, Shad Helmstetter says, "Make the decision to do what you choose, and your next step will be your own. Sit back and let the outside world take the lead and it will. Decide to determine your own next step—and thereby your future—and you can."

What's your next step? Think about it, ask for advice, and seek input from whatever higher power you rely on, but in the end, the decision to act or not act is yours. Staying where you are is easy because it doesn't require any effort, but getting to the next level requires doing things a little differently—and it starts with you deciding and becoming today what you want to be tomorrow.

There has never been a greater time for you to decide who you are becoming. You won the life lottery if you are in a position where you have the ability, time, and energy to read this book and use your mind to reflect on these ideas. Regardless of what's going on in your life, I'm sure you can find people who would love to switch places with you.

Don't take your life for granted.

Carve out some quiet time to think and consciously decide what type of human "being" you want to be.

The Solution

There's a scene in the film, The Matrix, where Neo, the main character, downloads into his brain a software program, which instantly gives him the ability to be a Kung Fu master. For now, there's no easy button for life.

But something I've noticed is that when you choose to take the easy road, your journey becomes harder. But when you choose the harder path, life becomes easier. Notice how I said "easier" and not "easy," because this doesn't mean a problem-free existence. Problems will always come, and life will eventually punch you in the mouth. But when you decide to be a Leader by Choice instead of by chance, you will live with more purpose, passion, and perseverance. And these are the ingredients that will help you not only survive but thrive during your most difficult challenges.

Becoming a Leader by Choice puts you on a difficult journey because it means you are intentional about taking responsibility for the things you can control—your attitude, your effort, your vision, and your personal (and spiritual) growth—at all times, regardless of your circumstances. It means you're living up to new standards that come from intentional decisions.

Isn't it great knowing you've been given the opportunity to choose your story, be self-aware, and take on your personal mission? Isn't it liberating to know you are not a victim of your circumstances?

All this time you have been empowered by your experiences, but it takes a new perspective to see it. Just like a person who needs to adjust the prescription on their eyeglasses, all of us will need to adjust our perspective continuously to ensure we can see clearly.

We've talked about so many concepts and ideas, but they were all focused on one thing—helping you become a Leader by Choice so you can intentionally live a successful, intentional, and purpose-based life by choice and not chance. It's a life-long process, so don't rush it because it's in the daily process itself that you are being shaped and molded.

Implementation

I've never read anything from Shakespeare, but I'm reminded of the quote from the play Hamlet, "To be, or not to be; that is the question." I don't know if this is what Shakespeare had in mind when he wrote this, but to be the person you want to become, you have a choice: to be or not to be. In other words, to be or "being" is something that you are continuously, so to become something, you get to decide to be it now, in the present. Today.

It's a choice you consciously make every day.

Amy Cuddy, an American psychologist who studies discrimination, nonverbal communication, and its effects on the mind has a TED Talk that's been viewed nearly 40 million times. One of the things her research supports is the idea of being that person you want to become. So instead of "faking it 'til you make it," Cuddy takes it one step further and says, "Fake it 'til you become it."[43]

Convince yourself that you are a Leader by Choice. Leading yourself through the seven decisions we discussed. When you start acting like a Leader by Choice, you will start to think and feel differently, and people will notice a change in you—and then they will treat you differently, which will reinforce who you are and who you are becoming.

Be it before you feel it. Be a Leader by Choice. You're ready.

ACKNOWLEDGMENTS

- To Jesus Christ for giving me a model for servant leadership and for being the most important decision I made in my life.
- To my wife for putting up with me during the writing of this book, for all her support, and for giving me some free time.
- To my daughters for being my "why."
- To my abuela for constantly asking why it was taking me so long to write this book.
- To Kendall Ficklin for being my kick in the pants.
- To Farnoosh Brock for giving me the idea to write this book and for introducing me to the side hustle.
- To Kingsley Grant for the mentoring.
- To Scott Dinsmore (R.I.P.) and The Live Your Legend community.
- To Kary Obberbrunner for writing great books and letting me participate in his journey.
- To Erick Thomas, Carle, and CJ for pushing me to win.
- To Aunt Jane and Rose for introducing me to the world of art and higher learning.
- To Clare Cole and Gina Mangarella for proofreading.

NOTES

Introduction

1. Tyson, Mike. Quotation retrieved from The Sun Sentinel newspaper   http://articles.sun-sentinel.com/2012-11-09/sports/sfl-mike-tyson-explains-one-of-his-most-famous-quotes-20121109_1_mike-tyson-undisputed-truth-famous-quotes

2. Ziglar, Zig. Quotation retrieved from the Ziglar website. https://www.ziglar.com/quotes/money-will-buy-you-bed/

3. Pressfield, Steven. Quotation retrieved from list of quotes from his books found on Good Reads. http://www.goodreads.com/quotes/576175-most-of-us-have-two-lives-the-life-we-live

Chapter 1

4. Bannister, Roger. Quotation retrieved from The Guardian. https://www.theguardian.com/sport/2004/apr/26/athletics

5. Brown, Les. Quotation retrieved from Awaken The Greatness Within.http://awakenthegreatnesswithin.com/50-inspirational-les-brown-quotes/

6. Ziglar, Zig. Quotation from Forbes Online https://www.forbes.com/sites/kevinkruse/2012/11/28/zig-ziglar-10-quotes-that-can-change-your-life/#6634592226a0

Chapter 2

7. Darwin, Charles. Source of the unconfirmed, but most associated with Charles Darwin. http://quoteinvestigator.com/2014/05/04/adapt/

8. Drucker, Peter. Retrieved from an article, which was published as a book titled Managing Oneself by Peter Drucker.

9. Godin, Seth. Quote retrieved from Seth Godin's blog. http://sethgodin.typepad.com/seths_blog/2010/01/quieting-the-lizard-brain.html

10. Thurman, Howard. African-American theologian, philosopher, Civil Rights Activist, and education.

https://www.goodreads.com/author/quotes/56230.Howard_Thur
man

11. Franklin, Benjamin. Quote retrieved from Benjamin Franklin
    appearing in the 1750 issue of Poor Richard's Almanac.
12. www.LiveYourLegend.com. A community started by Scott
    Dinsmore to help people find and do work they love.

Chapter 3

13. Ridely, Matt. Quote retrieved from Reader's Digest an
article titled "17 Reasons It's A Great Time To Be Alive"
http://www.rd.com/health/healthy-eating/cheer-up-17-reasons-its-a-
great-time-to-be-alive/

14. Ericsson, Anders K. Article in the Harvard Business
Review titled "The Making of An Expert"
https://hbr.org/2007/07/the-making-of-an-expert

15. Seligman, Martin. Quote from quote directory AZ
Quotes.
http://www.azquotes.com/quote/845168

16. Osteen, Joel. Book "Every Day a Friday"

Chapter 4

17. Drucker, Peter. Quote retrieved from an article in the Harvard Business Review book titled "On Leadership: HBR's 10 Must Reads." The article is titled "What Makes An Effective Executive"

18. Maxwell, John. Quote retrieved from John Maxwell's website in his about page.
http://www.johnmaxwell.com/about/meet-john/

19. Welch, Jack. Quote retrieved from Good Read's page with quotes from Jack Welch's books.
https://www.goodreads.com/work/quotes/856917-winning

20. Maxwell, John. Quote retrieved from the book "Be A People Person: Effective Leadership Through Effective Relationships"

21. Washington, Booker. Quote retrieved from Leadership Now blog post.
http://www.leadershipnow.com/leadingblog/2011/02/the_wisdom_o f_booker_t_washing.html

Chapter 5

22. Goins, Jeff. Quote retrieved from Jeff Goin's website. http://goinswriter.com/portfolio-life/

23. Frankl, Victor. Quote retrieved from book: "Man's Search For Meaning" by Victor Frankl page 131

24. Statistics come from two sources: https://www.ncbi.nlm.nih.gov/pubmed/16080587 http://www.nytimes.com/2006/03/14/health/14real.html

25. Goins, Jeff. Quote comes from "The Art of Work: A Proven Path To Discovering What You Were Meant To Do" by Jeff Goins

26. Brock, Farnoosh is the author, speaker, coach and owner of Prolific Living. www.Prolificliving.com

27. Rohn, Jim. Quote retrieved from book "5000+ Quotes For The Seeker of Riches."

28. King, Martin Luther. Quote comes a speech given *in Detroit, June 23,*

*1963(http://www.quotationspage.com/quote/24968.html)*http://www.
businessinsider.com/commit-to-something-to-find-your-calling-
2015-4

29. Goins, Jeff. Quote retrieved from Jeff Goins article on
Business Insider.
http://www.businessinsider.com/commit-to-something-to-find-your-
calling-2015-4

Chapter 6

30. Dweck, Carol. Quote retrieved from an article written in
The Glossary of Education Reform
http://edglossary.org/growth-mindset/

31. Statistics come from article written by the Real Buzz
Team
https://www.realbuzz.com/articles/10-shocking-gym-statistics/

32. Statistics come from Toyota's Press release.
http://toyotanews.pressroom.toyota.com/releases/toyota+corolla+40
+million+sold.htm

33. Statistics were retrieved from an article in I Am
Publishing.

https://www.iamselfpublishing.com/90-americans-want-to-write-a-book/

Chapter 7

34. Williams, Richard. Quote retrieved from an article written for CNN by Don Riddel and Gary Morley. http://edition.cnn.com/2015/09/11/tennis/richard-williams-serena-venus-tennis/

35. Duckworth, Angela. Quote retrieved from a TED talk given by Angela Duckworth. The exact quote can be found at the 3:01 mark. https://www.ted.com/talks/angela_lee_duckworth_grit_the_power_of_passion_and_perseverance/transcript?language=en

36. Bible scripture was retrieved from the New International Version (NIV) in the Book of Matthew verse 5:45

37. Duckworth, Angela. Quote retrieved from the Quote Catalog. https://quotecatalog.com/quote/angela-duckworth-but-when-they-l-b1rOOM7

38. Matthews, Michael. Quote retrieved from article titled "How To Quickly Gain Muscle"

https://www.muscleforlife.com/how-to-quickly-gain-muscle/

39. Quote from the website of the Center For Disease Control's page on Drug Overdoses.

www.cdc.gov/drugoverdose

40. Obberbrunner, Kary. Quote retrieved from the book The Deeper Path.

The Deeper Path by Kary Obberbrunner

41. Explanation of Purple Heart was found in Wikipedia.

https://en.wikipedia.org/wiki/Purple_Heart"Being wounded or killed in any action against an enemy of the United States or as a result of an act of any such enemy or opposing armed forces."

42. Bible scripture comes from the New International Version.

The book of Psalms verse 90:12

Conclusion

43. Cuddy, Amy. Quote retrieved from TED talk. The quote takes place at 19:15 mark.

https://www.ted.com/talks/amy_cuddy_your_body_language_shapes_who_you_are

LOOKING FOR A SPEAKER OR COACH? BRING ANDRES' UNIQUE INTERNATIONAL LEADERSHIP EXPERIENCE INTO YOUR ORGANIZATION

SPEAKER|AUTHOR| KICK-IN-THE-PANTS

Choosing the right speaker for your organization can be challenging. Andres' leadership message is authentic, inspirational, and PRACTICAL. Each message is tailored to the needs and objectives of that organization.

"I don't have all the answers, but I have the questions that can help you make better decisions faster.»

Let's Connect :
www.AndresValdes.com
info@andresvaldes.com

Or join the community here:
https://www.facebook.com/groups/leaderbychoice/

Made in the USA
Columbia, SC
17 November 2017